Acoustic Guitar Techniques

For

Songwriters

VOLUME ONE

Todd Ferris Mosby

ISBN-13:978-1463537333
BISAC: Music/Instruction & Study/Songwriting

Copyright © 2011 *Todd Ferris Mosby & Mosby Music Group*

All rights reserved. The owner of this book
may make copies for their own use. Other
portions may not be reproduced in any form
without written permission from the publisher.

Photos: Front Cover-Todd ferris Mosby,
Inside Author Photo-Parker S. Mosby,
Inside Photos: Todd Ferris Mosby

Quotes: www.musicthoughts.com

Published by Mosby Music Group,
3 Waverton, St. Louis, Mo 63124
Email: mosby@mosbymusicgroup.com
Web: www.mosbymusicgroup.com

"*Practice Nicely!*" - *Ustadt Imrat Khan*

About The Author:

Todd Ferris Mosby has authored three method books for Guitar and is a Professor of Guitar at Maryville University in St. Louis, Mo. He has composed for theater, feature film, television, concert stage, and given performances regionally, nationally and internationally.

His education includes Composition and Arranging at Berklee College of Music, Music Business at Fontbonne University, private instruction in classical North Indian Music under Ustadt Imrat Khan, private composition under Dr. Roland Jordan and advanced guitar studies under Fareed Haque.

Todd Mosby is an adjunct faculty member in Maryville University's music department. He has established himself as a refined guitarist, and also a dedicated and highly systematic teacher. His method book *Acoustic Guitar Techniques For Songwriters Volume 1* illustrates both the extent of Todd's devotion to teaching and the concentrated thought he has given to the art of guitar pedagogy.

I have no doubt that guitarists will find this manual a valuable tool.

Peter Henderson, D.M. Assistant Professor of Music & Director of Music, Maryville University (Saint Louis, Missouri).

"The layout and presentation of this book is well thought out, methodical and easy to follow. Any student at any level will find it easy to access." - Dr. Roland Jordan, Composer in Residence, Washington University, St. Louis, Mo.

"I was able to teach an 8 year old the E Minor Pentatonic Scale in 10 minutes using this method."
Alex Beck

"I actually learn to create music and songs rather than just play them."
Joanie Logue

Special Thanks:
To my teachers Dr. Roland Jordan and Ustadt Imrat Khan for their insights and support, my students and my parents.

*There's nothing worse
than a brilliant beginning.*

- Pablo Picasso -

INTRODUCTION

Thank you for taking the time to purchase and use this manual. Open-position playing on acoustic guitar is one of the most beautiful aspects of the instrument yet one of the least understood or even explored. The sounds emanating from this region of the instrument are truly expansive and emotionally expressive in a way which opens huge sonic doorways for placing your chords, melodies and licks.

The open position is also the area from which all other moveable forms evolve. The open strings provide a beauty and resonance which brings out the natural acoustic properties of your acoustic instrument. Few have ever really developed and mastered this aspect of guitar playing. As a matter of fact, the open position is one of the two areas higher level players tend to skim over once the moveable fingerings and chords are conquered.

This is where most beginning level players start. It is also where more advanced songwriters are lacking in a knowledge base geared to move them past the basic I - IV - V chord shapes. The really cool sounds are in easy reach if you understand the simple similarities of how these chords are built.

This is a very methodical text book style approach to learning your instrument in relation to songwriting which covers all aspects of right hand, left hand coordination, counting, rhythm and modern chord theory for the beginning thru Intermediate levels. Volume 1 provides the base which leads to Volume 2. Volume 2 takes the songwriter thru the more advanced levels of guitar technique, modern harmony and avanced open-string chord building.

For this reason I have compiled Volume 1 which explores the beauty of open-position with relative ease. The information is well thought out, tested and presented from a player's perspective. It gets right to how these chords and scales work with fail safe methods for learning them quickly so they can work for you.

Enjoy!

Todd Ferris Mosby
www.toddferrismosby.com

TABLE OF CONTENTS

PART ONE: *Fundamentals and Open-String Studies*

CHAPTER 1 - *Beginning Topics*
- Plugging In The Guitar 2
- Holding The Guitar 2
- Left Hand 4
- Right Hand 5
- Picking 6
- Tuning 6
- Guitar Chord Frames 7
- Note Names 8
- Time Signature 9
- Notation Values 13
- Three Chord Types 15
- Ascending Intervals - major & perfect 16

CHAPTER 2 - *Strumming Studies*
- Rhythm Guitar #1 18
- Dynamics 20
- Dividing String Groups 22
- Counting Even Rhythms 23
- Graduated Rhythms 25
- Finding Home Base 26
- Open String Groupings 27
- Rhythm Guitar #2 - *Basic Strum Patterns* 28

CHAPTER 3 - *Picking Studies*
- String Names 30
- Single String Down Up 31
- Counting Quarter Notes 32
- Counting Eighth Notes 34
- Counting Sixteenth Notes 35
- About Metronomes 35
- Picking Across 2 Adjacent Strings 38
- Picking Across 3 Adjacent Strings 41

PART TWO: *Open-Position Scale Studies*

CHAPTER 4 - *C Major Scale Studies-Open Position*
- Natural Major Scale 46
- Left Hand (LH) Right Hand (RH) 48
- LH 1/2 RH Even Subdivisions 49-52
- LH 1/4 RH Even Subdivisions 54-55
- LH 1/8 RH Even Subdivisions 56
- LH 1/16 RH 1/16 57
- Speed Study 58
- Groups of Three 59
- Groups of Four 60
- Chromatic Scale 61
- About Music 63

CHAPTER 5 - *Eminor Pentatonic & E Blues Scale Studies*
- Eminor Pentatonic Scale 65
  - Speed Study 67
  - Groups of Two 68
  - Groups of Three 68
  - Groups of Four 69
- E Blues Scale 70
  - Speed Study 72
  - Groups of Three 73
  - Groups of Four 74
- 12 Bar Blues in E 75
  - Blues Soloing Study 76
  - Two Measure Phrases 77

PART THREE: *Chordal Studies*

Chapter 6 - *Chords Part 1 - Open-Position*
- Power Chords 80
  - Studies 81-82
- Eight Open Position Chords 83
- Chord Transition Formulas 85
- Six Major Chords 88
- Horizontal Chord Movement 89
- Practice Progressions #1 91-94

i

Rhythm Guitar #3- *Folk Strum 1* 95
Modern Chord Theory-*Diatonic Harmony* 97
Practice Progressions #2 - *(I-IV-V, V-I, I-IV-bVII-IV)* 99-101

Chapter 7 - *Chords Part 2 - Open-Position*
Rhythm Guitar #4 - *Rock Ballad* 103
Practice Progressions #3 - *Common Chrd Patts* 104
Nine Open Position Chords 106
Practice Progressions #4 107
Special Case Chords - *Vertical Alignment* 110
Rhythm Guitar #5 - *Boom-Chick* 111
Special Case Chords - *Horizontal Alignment* 112
Practice Progressions #5 113
Introduction To Barre Forms 114

SUPPLEMENT CHAPTERS

Chapter 8 - *Rhythm Guitar Workouts*
Rhythm Workout #1 117
1/4 Note Studies 117
Tied Note Studies 118
1/8 Note Studies 120
Practice Progressions #6 122
B maj, B7, Bmin Chords 124

Chapter 9 - *Introduction To Finger Picking*
Right Hand Positioning 127
Groupings 130
Forward Activation 132
Arc Activation 134
Carcassi Activation 135

Chapter 10 - *Practice Tunes*
Various 138-175

Index
Quick Study reference Guide i
Sample Practice Sessions v
Basic Notation For Song Writing vi
Song Form #1 viii
Song Form #2 ix

iv

HOW TO USE THIS BOOK

Volume One is the first of a two volume series to help expand the songwriters palette in terms of guitar technique and songwriting ability. Volume One is devoted to building a strong foundation for Right Hand Left Hand technique, counting, sight reading chord charts, note sequencing and ability to interchange the Eight Open-Position Chords with ease.

Volume One is separated into three parts. Part One deals with fundamentals, terminology and open-string studies. Part Two addresses scale studies for the most common open-position scales. Part Three is introduces open-position chords along with studies to build transition technique.

Start from the beginning and go straight thru to the end of the book or go half way into Part One, go half way into Part Three, finish Part One , go half way into Part Two, finish Part Three, etc. Learn the note names on the instrument and apply to the staff as soon as possible. It may take some time but well worth the effort.

Take your time, there is no rush. Music is a very patient art form. It is always there waiting and wanting to reveal itself at the deeper levels. The more fluent you are with the note spellings in relation to scales, chord structure and placement on your instrument, the quicker the mysteries unfold. Please do not hesitate to find a qualified teacher/mentor for clraification on any aspect of the material.

PART ONE

Fundamentals & Open-String Studies

CHAPTER 1

Beginning Topics

*Music is the art of
thinking with sounds.*

- Jules Combariue -

PLUGGING IN THE GUITAR

Follow these steps when plugging your guitar into your amp in order to protect your equipment.

1. Turn the amp off and set the guitar volume and amp volume to 0.
2. Plug your 1/4" cable into your guitar and then into the amp.
3. Turn the amp on.
4. Turn the guitar volume all the way to 10.
5. Turn the amp volume up carefully until you reach the desired loudness.

HOLDING THE GUITAR

The guitar should be in the same position in relation to your body whether standing or sitting. This allows for consistent training of the right hand and left hand. It let's you keep the same hand position all the time and streamlines the learning curve.

The neck of the guitar should be parallel to approximately 45 degrees to the floor. This will automatically align the right hand in relation to the strings and sound hole. The back of the guitar should lean against the lower part of the chest. The height and angle should always be consistent whether sitting or standing. Your hands should not support any weight, they need to be free to move.

For acoustic electric guitars, always use a strap while sitting and set it so that the guitar is in a consistent position from sitting to standing. We want to give the hands one way of operating. Rest the guitar on the right leg. A foot rest may make it more comfortable while seated also.

Parallel positioning to floor. Right hand strikes an arc which sweeps thru the middle of sound hole.

Holding the guitar properly means more stamina, better playing technique, better tone, and avoidance of injuries down the road. Have an experienced guitarist or better yet a person trained in the Alexander Method to check your alignments to make sure their is no blockage of flow in your movements.

LEFT HAND

The left hand presses the strings to sound the notes. It should never feel strained and and should remain comfortable and in alignment to the rest of the arm.

Try to hold the natural position of the left hand on the fingerboard. This is found by dropping the left hand to your side. Notice there are no bends in the hand. This is your natural hand position. Now, raising it to the neck of the guitar, try to maintain that same hand position.

The middle of the thumb presses slightly down and forward on the on the upper middle portion of the guitar neck to allow freedom of movement for the fingers. The fingers then are able to act like the hammers on a piano to initiate sound. There should be a slight gap from the bottom of the guitar neck to the curved index finger of the left hand.

The fingers are numbered Thumb (T), index (1), middle (2), ring (3), pinky (4).

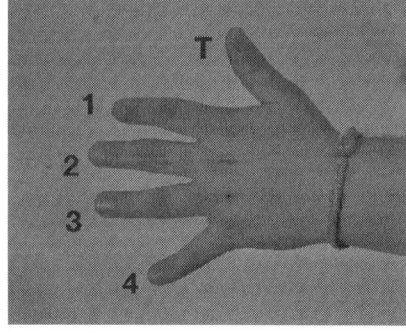
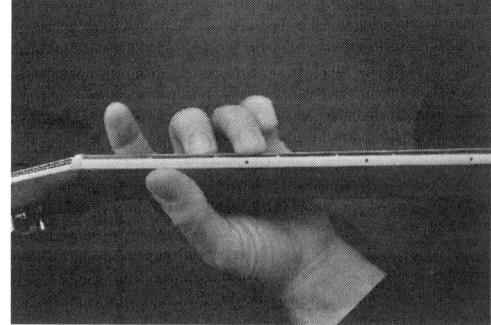

RIGHT HAND

Most jazz, rock, blues and bluegrass players use a pick. Picks help you play fast, clean notes and aid in certain aspects of strumming and chordal playing. Another word for pick is plectrum. This is the preferred style for players in these genres of music. It allows for a full spectrum of sound. Each pick has slightly different characteristics depending on shape, thickness and even wear.

Generally, the smaller the pick, the closer contact your fingers have to the strings.

Hold the pick between the middle of the thumb and first knuckle of your index finger. If you hold your right arm straight and parallel to the floor, the point of the pick should point to the floor. Use either the long side, flat side or both in the case of a down up strike to affect tone and glide across the strings. Hold the pick with a light touch, not so loose that it falls out and not so tight that there is a lot of tension.

Place your right forearm so it rests comfortably on the top front edge of the guitar. The forearm remains parallel to the face of the instrument. Use it as a fulcrum. In other words, the arm swings like a door or pendulum creating a slight angle across the strings as you sweep the pick from the 6th string to the 1st string. strike. The right hand will sweep an arc across the middle of the sound hole.

The fingers are numbered Thumb (p), index (i), middle (m), ring (a).

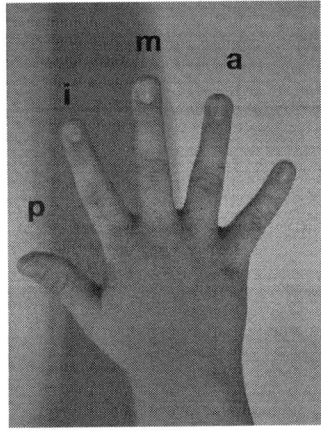
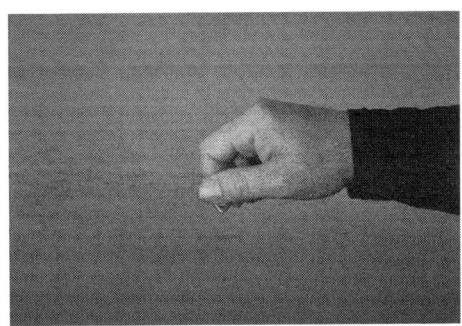

point of pick perpendicular to floor

PICKING A NOTE

Downstroke - Used for power and definition by most blues and rock players. When striking a string, move the pick downwards - not outwards - to strike the string. Let it rest on the string below. If on the first string, pretend there is an imaginary string below.

Upstroke - Used for emotive playing due to its expressive and warm sound. Strike the string upwards in the opposite direction with a flick of the wrist, minimal arm movement. Let it rest on the string above or a similar distance if on the 6th string.

Down-Up Stroke - Also called alternate picking, this stroke is used for speed. Keep the pick in as close to the string as possible. Once developed, gravity takes over giving a nice clicking sound and a velvety kind of touch.

TUNING

Always keep your guitar in good tune. The instrument gets used to the amount of tension on the wood making it easier to tune.

Tune your strings to the right notes. If the string is flat (too loose), tighten the tuning gear to increase tension. If the string is sharp (too tight), loosen the tuning gear to decrease tension. As you get close to the string being in tune, listen for the tiny beats or waves of sound which occur. When they disappear the string will be in tune. It will be like an Ah - Ha moment.

Guitar is the most difficult instrument to tune. As soon as one string increases in tension, the rest tend to shift in response. There are many ways to tune. An electronic tuner works well if you are already in the ball park.

5TH FRET TUNING

1. To tune the open 5th string, press the 6th string at the 5th fret.
2. To tune the open 4th string, press the 5th string at the 5th fret.
3. To tune the open 3rd string, press the 4th string at the 5th fret.
4. To tune the open 2nd string, press the 3rd string at the 4th fret.
5. To tune the open 1st string, press the 2nd string at the 5th fret.

Guitar Chord Frames

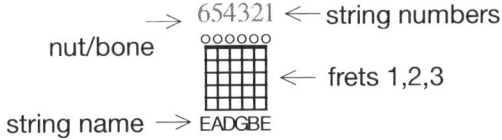

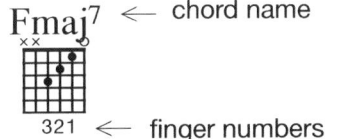

x: string not played
o: open string

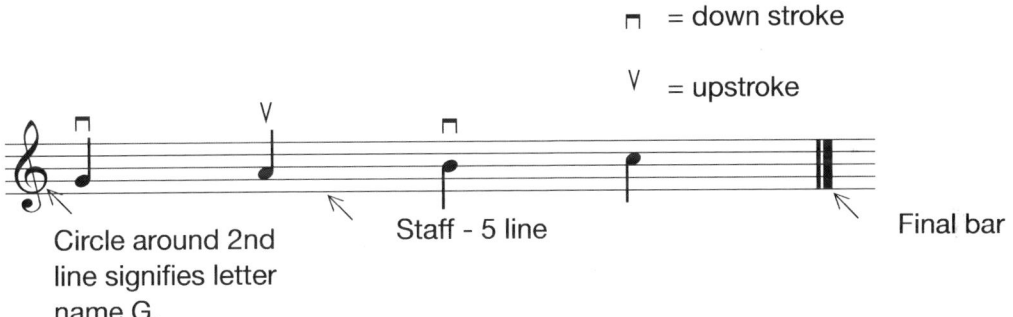

⊓ = down stroke

V = upstroke

Repeat Signs

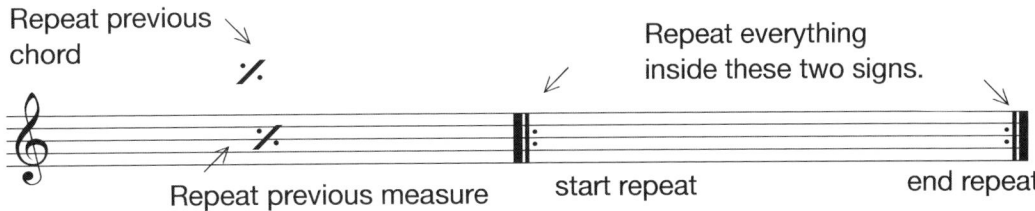

Study 1.1
Note Names

Notes on the staff - memorize

MUSICAL ALPHABET:
Memorize forward and backward. Only 7 letters but unlimited combinations when used with rhythm.

A B C D E F G

B C D E F G A

C D E F G A B

D E F G A B C

E F G A B C D

F G A B C D E

G A B C D E F

Time Signature

Time signature is the most cohesive aspect of music. It is the way in which we group, use and make sense of pulse. **Pulse** is the aspect of music which binds pitch and rhythm into a cohesive and repeating cycle.

We are consistently bombarded by pulse day and night while awake or asleep. The heart beats at a different rate from the kidneys which pulse at a different rate from the brain. Walk out side and the traffic is moving at different rates, conversation between people moves and pulses at different rates, music in a restaurant the list goes on.

What makes pulse work in a musical context?

As soon as we begin to group pulse in a consistent manner by **marking one**, thenrandom pulse can be placed in a useful musical context. Marking time like this in western music creates what is called a measure or bar.

A **measure** groups pulses into a repeating pattern. This can range anywhere from a count of two all the way to a count of four hundred. The most common pulse used western music is the quarter note pulse grouped in counts of four or 4/4 time. One repeats every four counts (1234, 1234, 1234).

Study 1.2
Time

4 *means: 4 counts/pulses per measure*

4 *means: quarter note pulse*

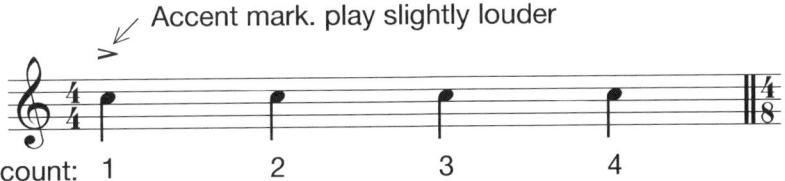

count: 1   2   3   4

4/8 is a faster eight note pulse,
same count.

count: 1   2   3   4

4/16 is a fast sixteenth note pulse,
same count.

count: 1   2   3   4

4/2 is a slower half note pulse,
same count.

count: 1   2   3   4

8/4 places pulses or counts into groups of eight.

count: 1   2   3   4   5   6   7   8

Study 1.3
Time Signature

TERMINOLOGY:

1) Let's play this tune in 3. Means play this song in 3/4 time.
2) Give me 4 bars of C maj in 4. Means play 4 measures of the C major chord in 4/4 time.
3) I will give 2 counts of four on the outside. Means count 2 measures of 4/4 time before starting the tune.
4) Let's take four for four. Means four measures in 4/4 time.

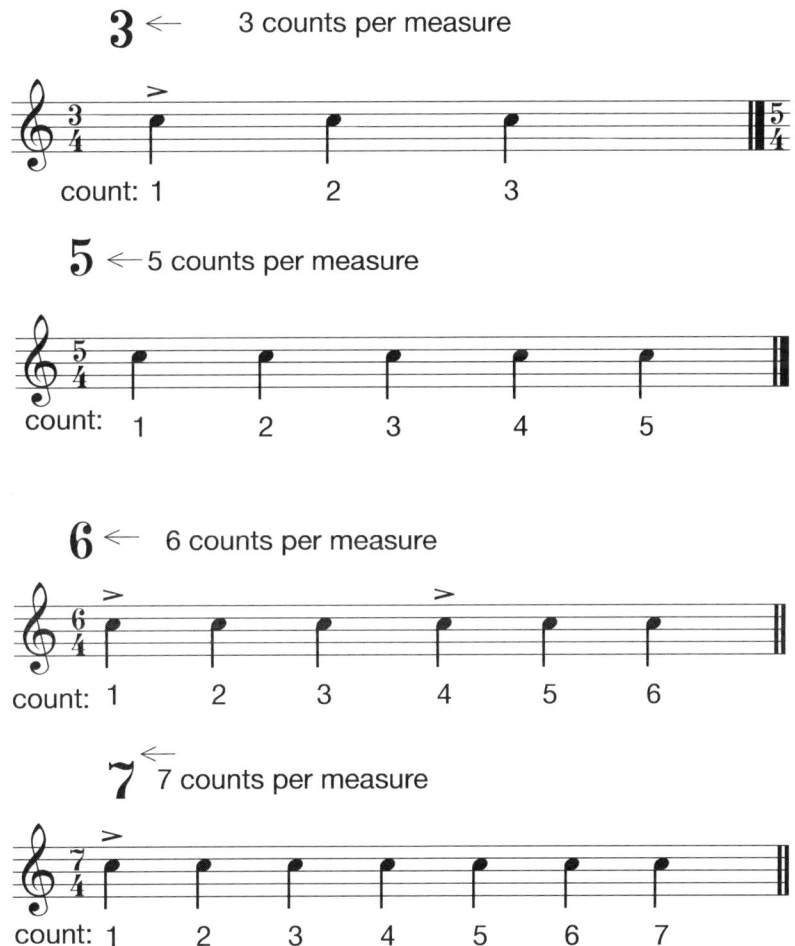

Study 1.4
Grouping Time

It is very easy to break down any thing higher than a count of four into various groupings. This works particularly well with odd time signatures.

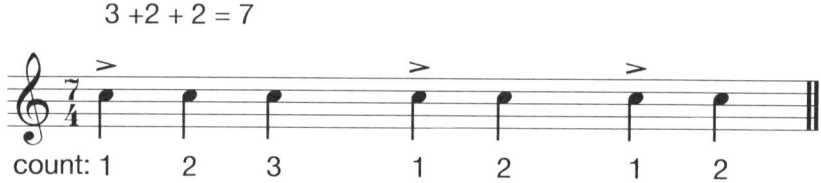

Study 1.5
Note Values

Study 1.6
Rhythm Guitar Note Values

Slash notation or percussion notation is used for rhythm guitar playing. Pulse is the internalization of a quarter-note tempo taken from an external source. Tap the heart area to bring body timing on line and generate an internal pulse.

Whole, half & quarter notes take either all down strokes or all up strokes. Eighth & sixteenth notes always take down-up strokes.

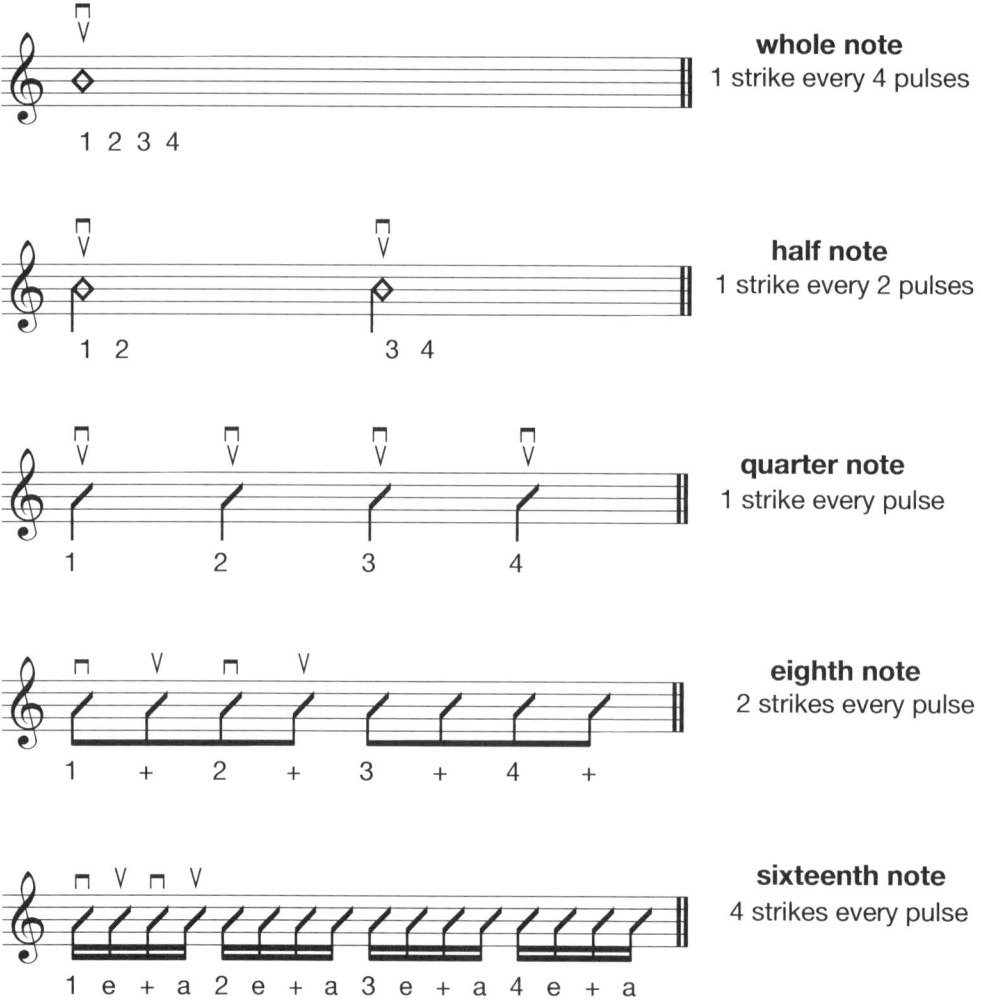

Three Chord Types

There are 3 types of chords which will be used in this presentation:
a) Power Chord, b) Open Chord, c) Barre Chord.

The Power chord is the quickest way to get tunes and progressions from recordings into your hands before transferring to the open and barre chords.

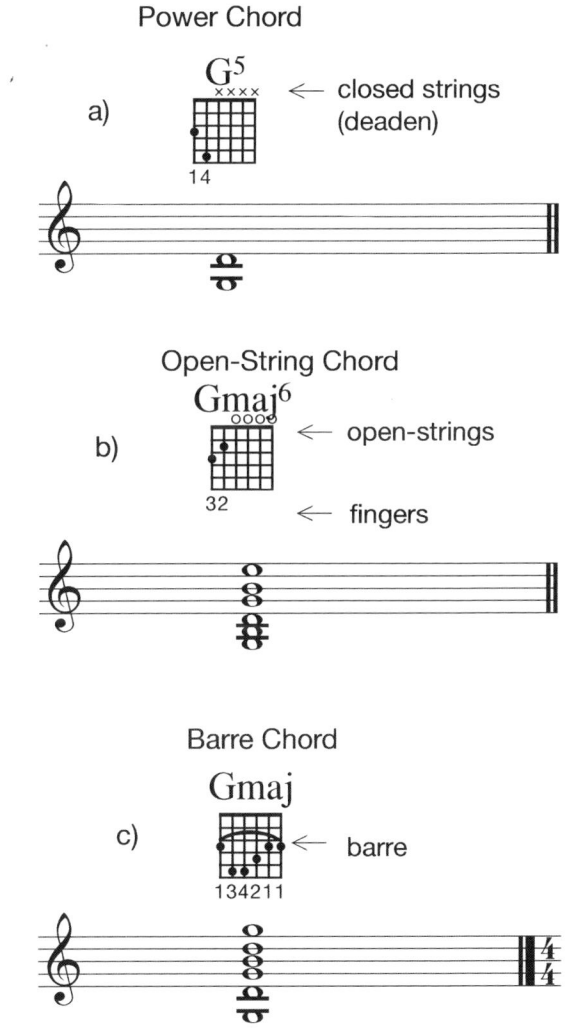

Study 1.7
Ascending Intervals - major & perfect

When learning intervals, it helps to place them with in the context of a well know tune.

RECOGNIZE & MEMORIZE

Major 2nd - Happy Birthday
Rudolf The Red Nose...

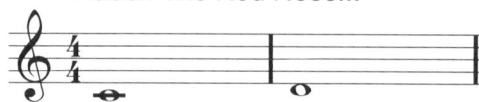

Major 3rd - Oh When The Saints...

Perfect 4th - Here Comes The Bride
Oh Christmas Tree

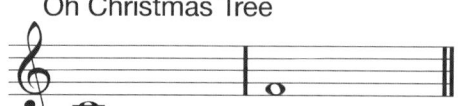

Perfect 5th - Twinkle Twinkle

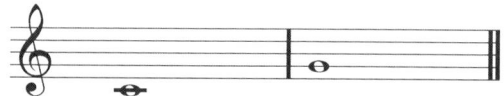

Major 6th - NBC
It Came Upon A Midnight Clear

Major 7th - Cast Your fate To The Wind

Perfect Octave - Somewhere Over The Rainbow
A Christmas Song (Chestnuts...)

CHAPTER 2

Strumming Studies
Open-String

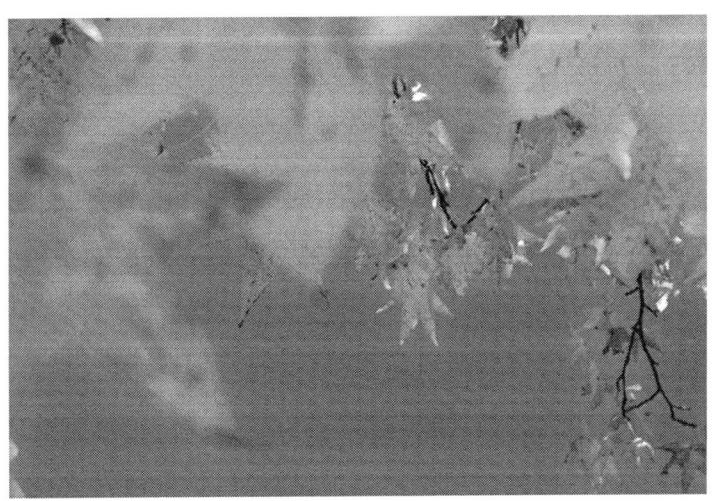

*If you don't make a mistake,
you're not trying hard enough.*

- Charlie Parker -

RHYTHM GUITAR #1

Balancing Down & Up Strokes

REMINDER:

a) The forearm covers the distance across the strings. Remain with in the imaginary string lines above and below the 1st and 6th strings.

b) Slight flicking of the wrist covers the speed at which the the pick bursts across the strings. We are trying to trick the ear into hearing it as one burst.

c) Try to retain consistent speed between the down strokes and up strokes.

d) Listen!

Strum using all 6 open strings.

a)

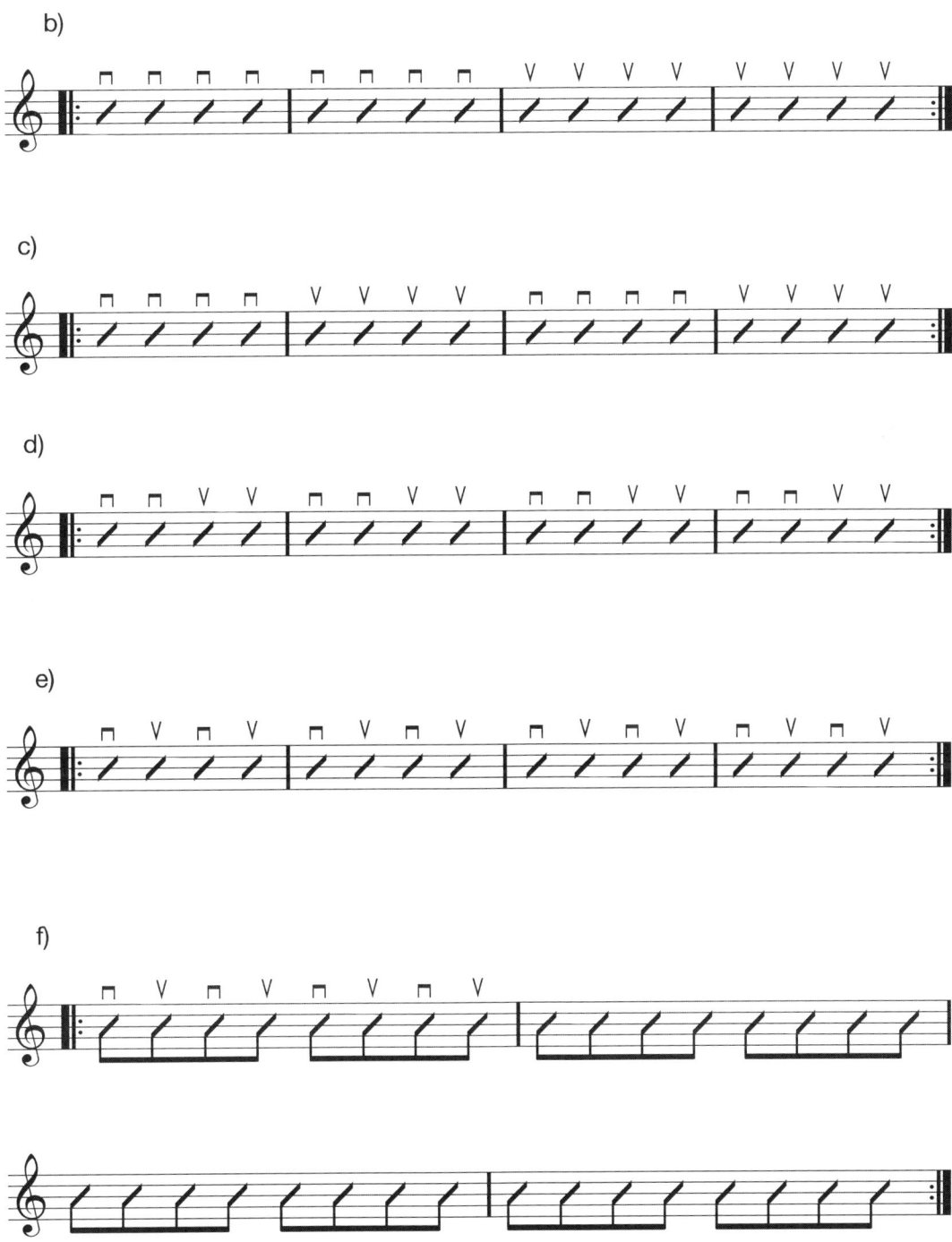

Study 2.1
Dynamics

Guitar has only 3 basic dynamic ranges - Loud, Soft and Moderate.

f **Loud** (forte) can be used for trying to catch attention in a large room or when emphasizing particular rhythms as in a shout or word stress.

p **Soft** (piano) can be used to bring the listener in as in a whisper.

m **Moderate** (moderate) is for normal playing as in a normal conversation level.

Guitar works with in a pretty narrow dynamic range.

Dynamics in music follow much of the same dynamic rules found in language. Whether playing thru a large sound systyem or a small living room, the dynamic range on guitar remains relatively the same.

Maintain a consistent speed through out. Play all 6 open strings.

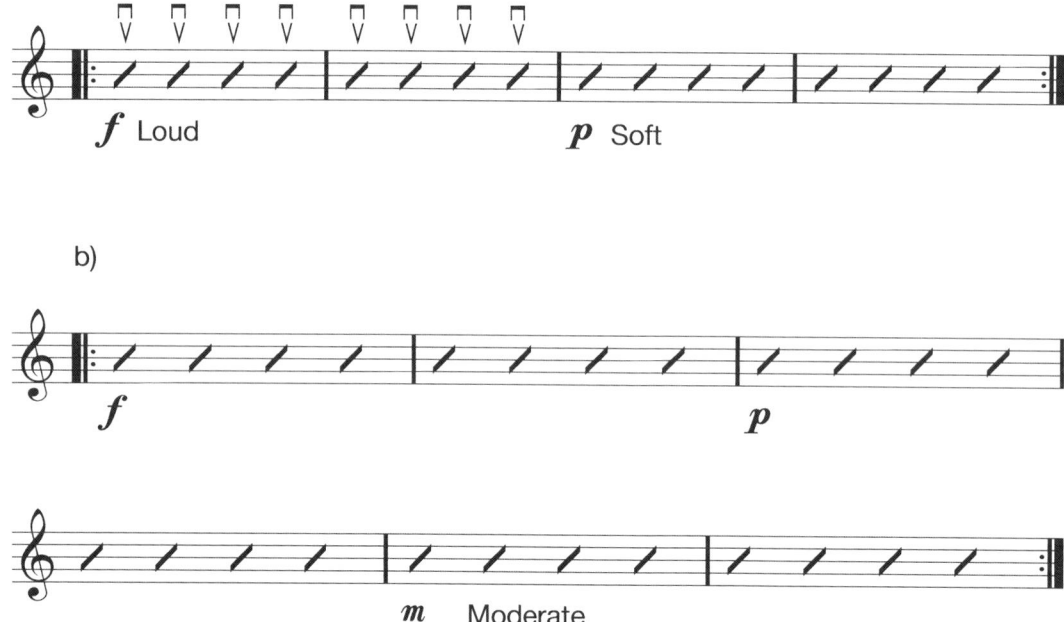

REMINDER: Maintain same speed through out. Play all 6 open strings.
Maintain a feather like touch in right hand.

c)

f p m

d)

f p m f p m

e)

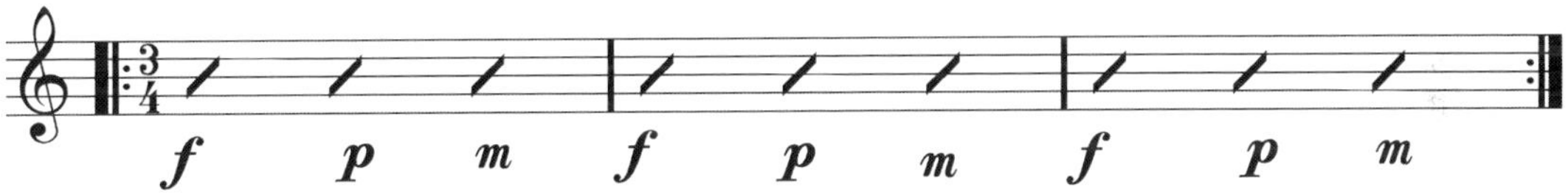

f p m f p m f p m

Study 2.2
Dividing String Groups

This exercise is to prepare your right for strumming different string sets.

1) Play as all downs.
2) Strike 8,4,2,1 times on each string set.
3) Use all quarter note values.
4) Increase tempo.

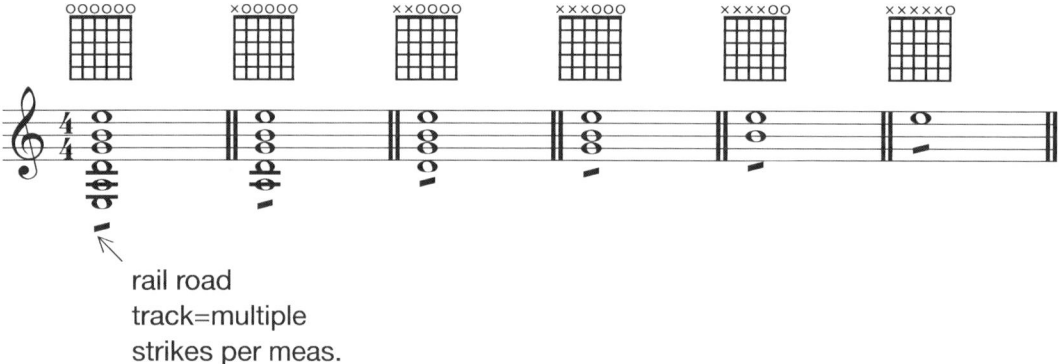

rail road track=multiple strikes per meas.

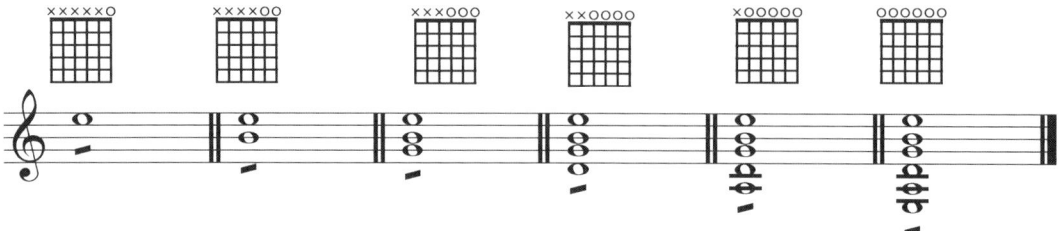

Study 2.3
Counting Even Rhythms

Strum 6 open strings.

REMEMBER:
1) Stay inside your imaginary string lines above and below the 1st and 6th strings.
2) Play Medium volume.
3) Right arm swing with slight wrist rotation.
4) Have all strings burst with even volume across strings.
5) Downstrokes and upstrokes equal in volume.
6) Always return to READY POSITION

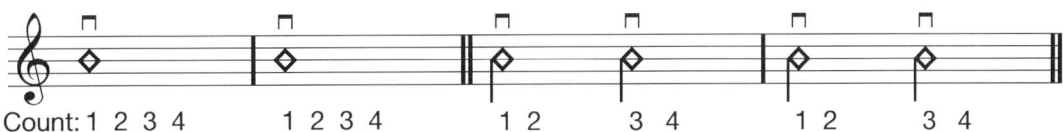

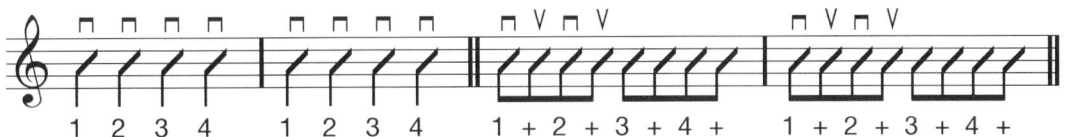

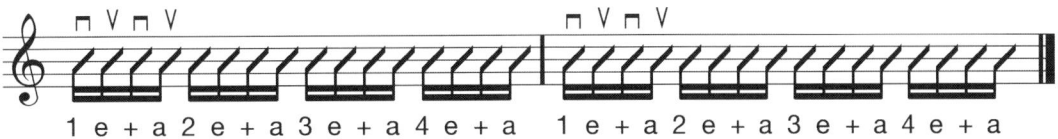

Study 2.4
Changing Rhythmic Values

Strumming and Counting between quarter note and eighth note values.
Repeat A & B as needed until you can play it without repeats.

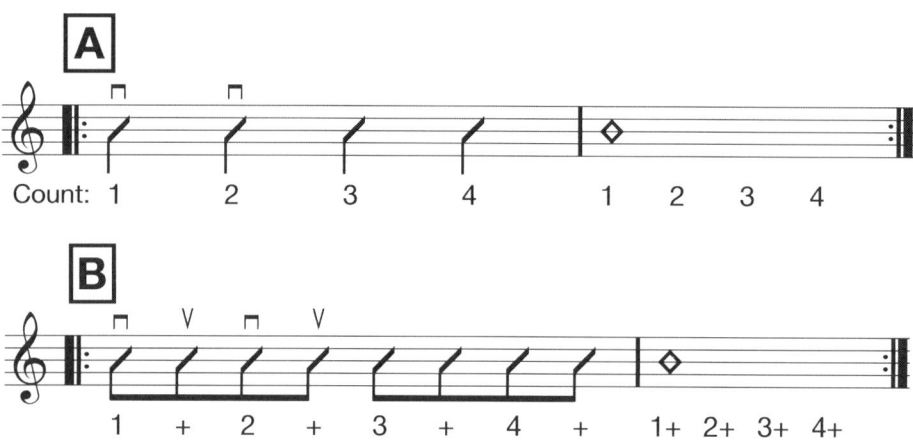

Strumming and Counting between 8th note and 16th note values.
Repeat C & D as needed until you can play it without repeats.

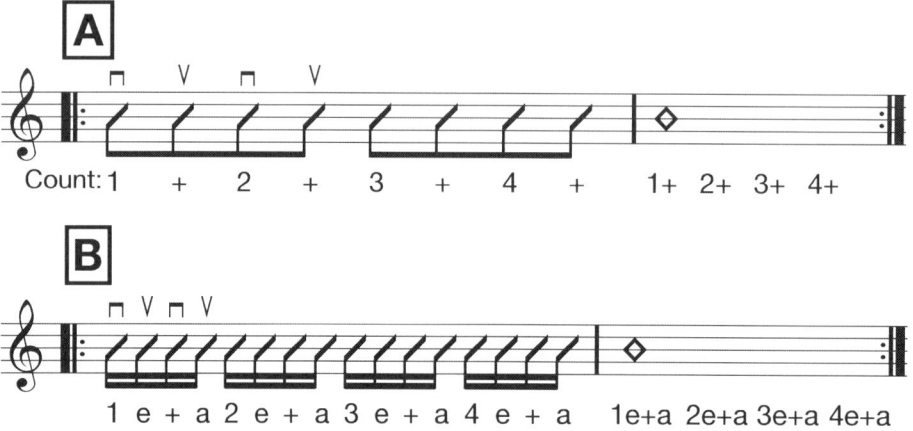

Study 2.5
Graduated Rhythms

Strum and Count consistently in 2 measure phrases throughout.
Use a metronome.

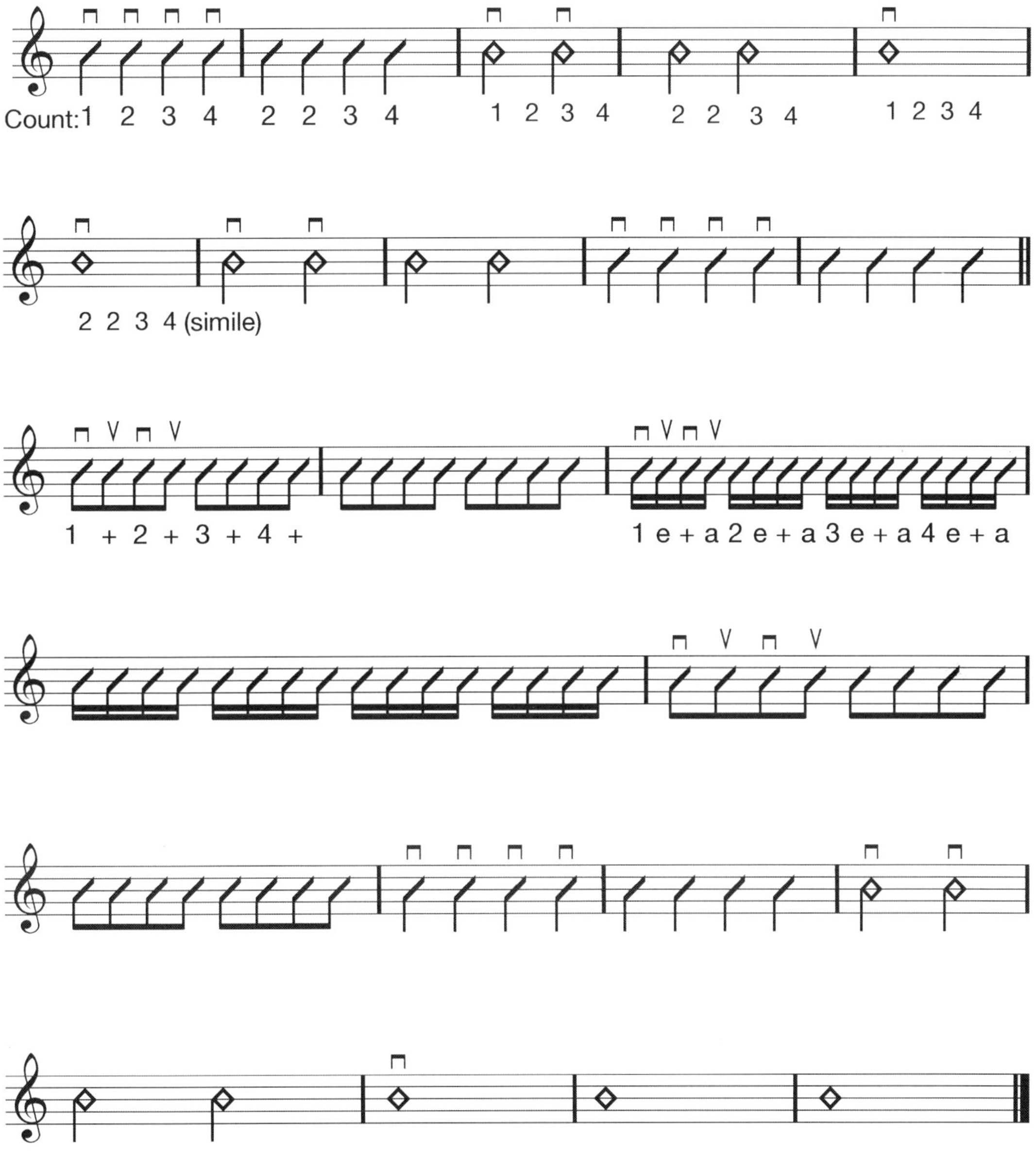

Count: 1 2 3 4   2 2 3 4   1 2 3 4   2 2 3 4   1 2 3 4

2 2 3 4 (simile)

1 + 2 + 3 + 4 +   1 e + a 2 e + a 3 e + a 4 e + a

Study 2.6
Finding Home Base

This is a strumming and counting game to see if you can maintain an even pulse throughout while shifting between the different rhythmic values at random. Start by finding a comfortable sixteenth note speed and then begin at any value.

1) Play each measure with and with out repeats. Remember the quarter note is like home base.

2) Once moving from whole note to sixteenth note is mastered can you move between 2 chords using the same exercise.

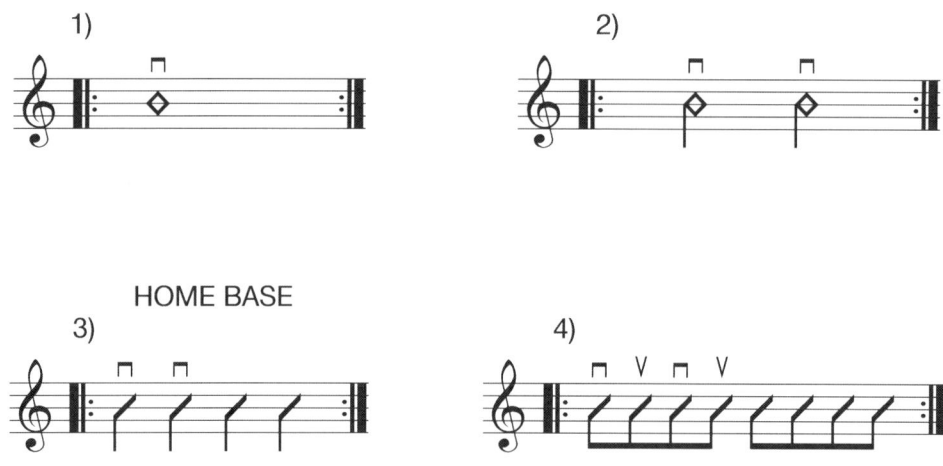

HOME BASE

Study 2.7
Open-String Groupings

27

Now play studies 2.1-2.6 with 5 and 4 string groupings. These groupings reflect the basic open-string chord groupings and must be mastered to accurately play the open string chords which I am presenting in this book.

O = open string.   X = closed string (do not play).

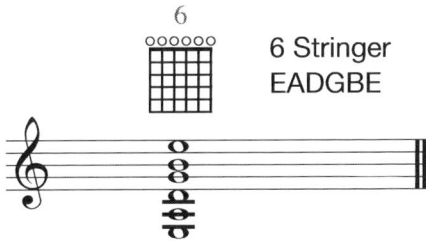

6 Stringer
EADGBE

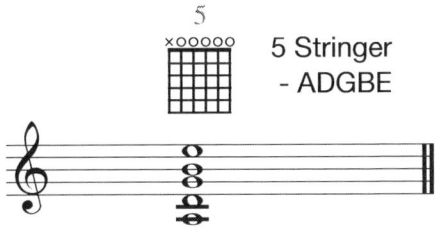

5 Stringer
- ADGBE

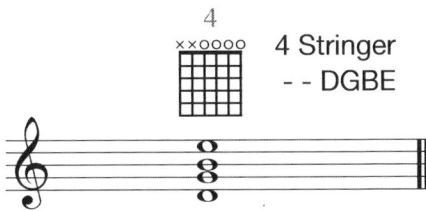

4 Stringer
- - DGBE

RHYTHM GUITAR #2

Basic Strum Patterns

These are the strum patterns that are used for 85% of the open chord playing in popular music. Be able to recognize and interchange these patterns freely and at will. Play with and without repeats.

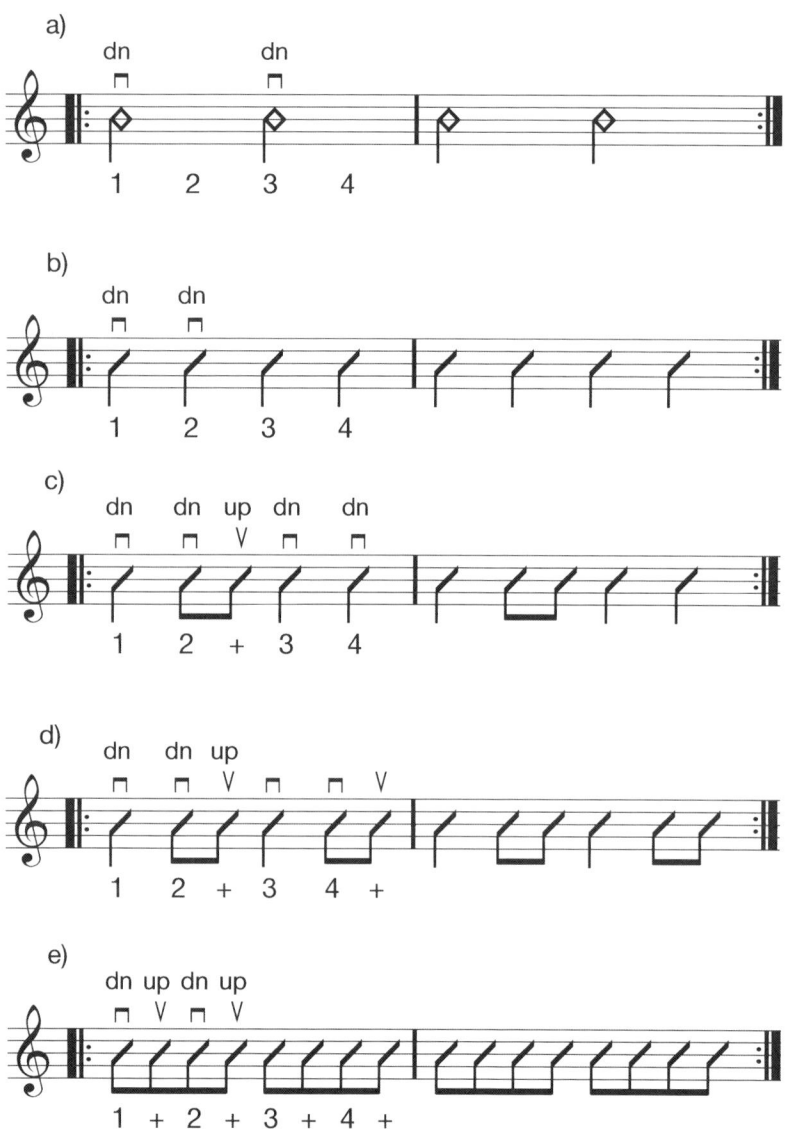

CHAPTER 3

Picking Studies
Open-String

*In writing songs
I've learned as much
from Cezanne as I have
from Woddie Gutherie.*

Bob Dylan

String Names

Picking on each individual open string allows the right hand muscles to really feel the true weight and mass of each string against the pick.

NOTE: Quarter notes strike thru to the adjacent string below. Eighth and sixteenth notes pick as close to string center as possible.

⑥ = string number

MEMORIZE

6TH & 5TH strings carry the root, 5th and 3rd of the chord.

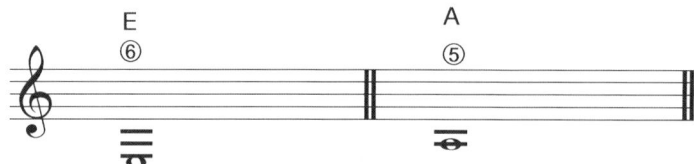

4TH & 3RD strings carry the 3rd & 7th of the chord.

2ND & 1ST strings carry the color tones of the chord.

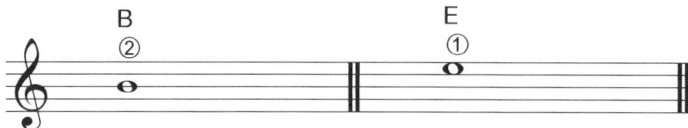

Study 3.1
Single-String Down/Up Strokes

⊓ = **down stroke**. Strike pick over the top of string into the next string below.

V = **up stroke**. Strike pick over the top of string into the next string above.

⊓ V = **down/up (alternate) stroke**. Keep pick in as close to center of string as possible. Let centrifugal force take over movement.

Let each note ring to its full value. Do not cut short!

Study 3.2
Counting Quarter Notes

Play each study with a metronomme.

b)

c)

d)

Study 3.3
Counting Eighth Notes

Continue in the same manner as Ex. 10 with eighth notes using only down up picking.

Keep counting in 2 measure phrases through out.

ABOUT METRONOMES

An eighth note at 120mm is the same speed as a sixteenth note at 60mm.
A sixteenth note at 60mm is the same speed as an eighth note at 120mm.
A quarter note at 240 is the same speed as an eighth note at 120.
Understand?

Study 2.4
Counting Sixteenth Notes

Continue in the same manner as Ex. 10 with sixteenth notes using only down up picking.

a)

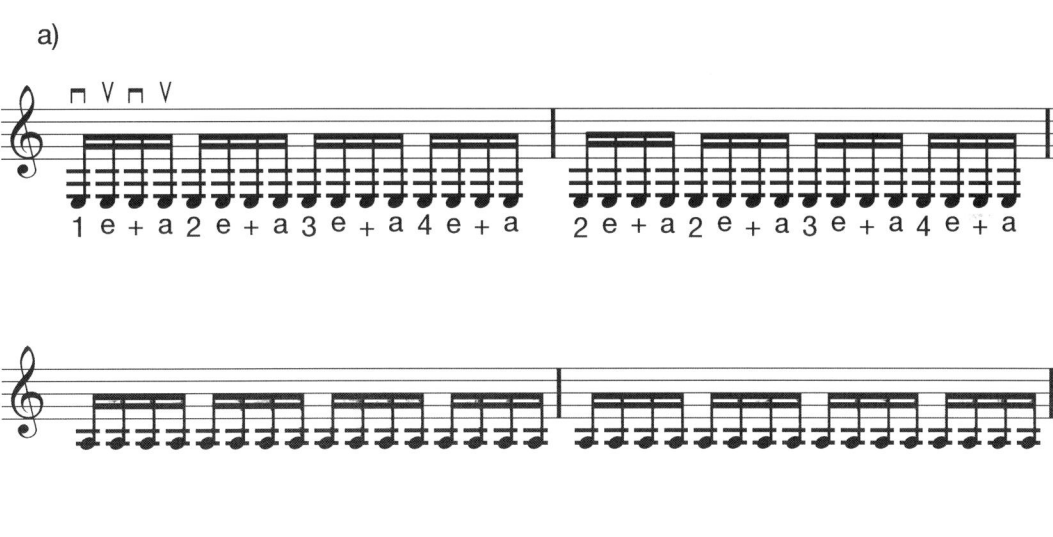

ascend/descend (etc.)

b)

c)

ascend/descend (etc.)

d)

ascend/descend (etc.)

e)

f)

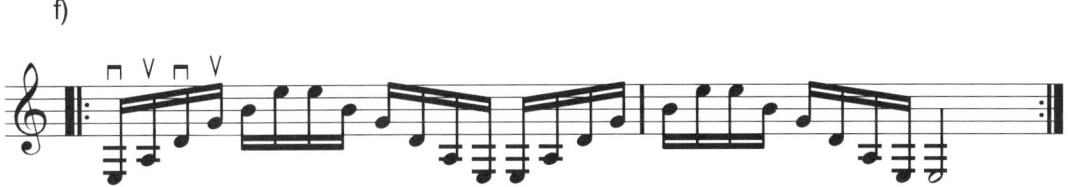

Can you find some cool open string color chords to use with this exercise?

Can you move between 2 chords every 2 measures? Every measure?

Can you use the pentatonic scale on these exercises?

Study 3.5
Picking Across Two Adjacent Strings

This exercise allows development of the right hand as it feels the picking distance of adjacent strings. Ascending the pick travels over a set of two strings. Descending the pick travels between a set of two strings.

This isolated movement is very important due to the fact all scales and pentatonics cross adjacent strings.

40

c)

Study 3.6
Picking Across Three Adjacent Strings

a)

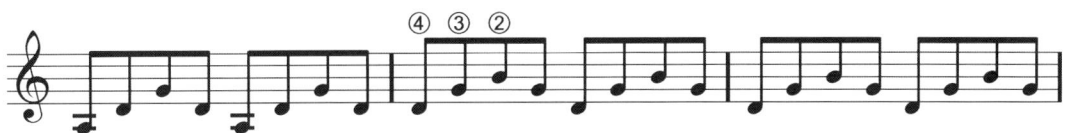

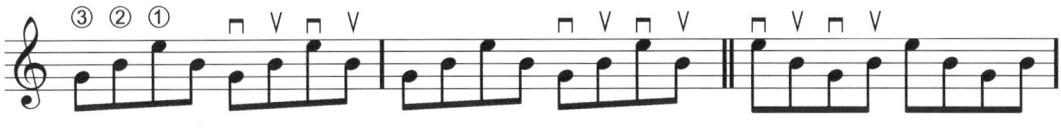

Can you find some cool open string color chords to use with this exercise?

Can you move between 2 chords every 2 measures? Every measure?

PART TWO

Open-Position Scale Studies

CHAPTER 4

Major Scale Studies
Open-Position

*I try to be prepared for the moment,
through understanding and
being warmed up,
knowing all about chords
and scales
so I don't even
have to think
and can get right
to what it is
I want to say.*

Pat Metheny

NATURAL MAJOR SCALE
Starting on E

1st fret takes first finger all strings, 2nd fret-2nd finger all strings, 3rd fret-3rd finger all strings, 4th fret-4th finger all strings.

Play each string until comfortable, out of time then in time. This approach allows memorization of all available note groupings in relation to each string.

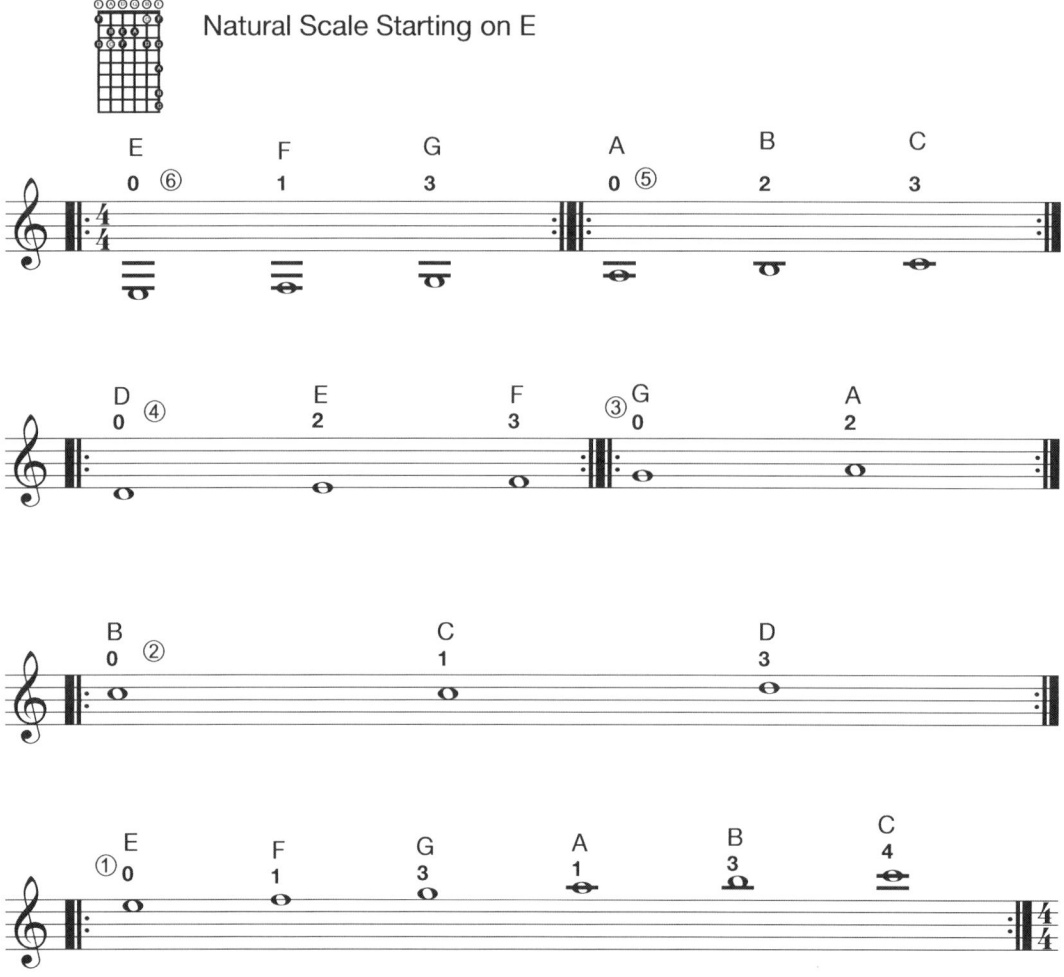

47

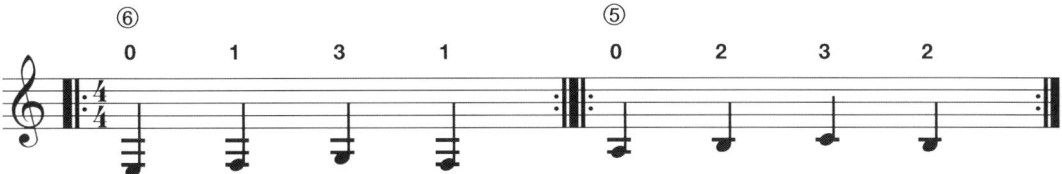

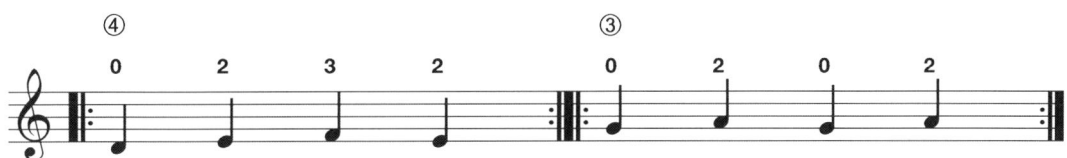

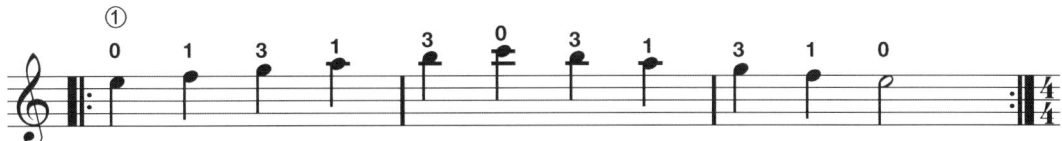

Study 4.1
Right Hand Left Hand

Let each note ring to its full value.

Study 4.2
LH Half - RH Half

This exercise develops LH (Left Hand) and RH (Right Hand) counting and performance accuracy on the even subdivisions. It also allows the LH to slow down enough for the mind to catch up with the notes.

NOTE: You are counting 5 measure groups.

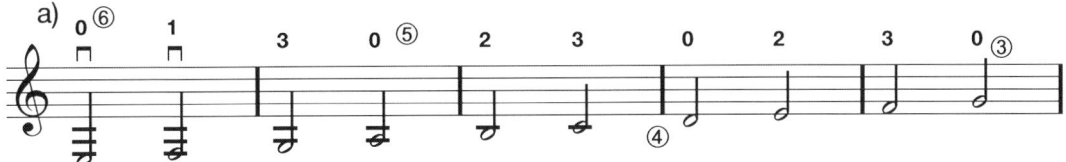

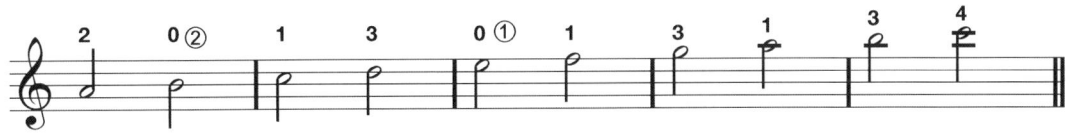

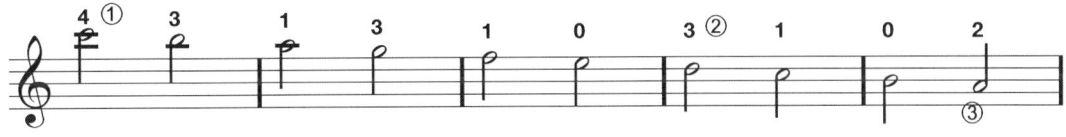

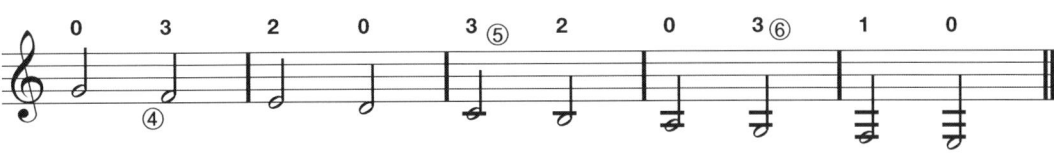

Study 4.3
LH Half - RH Quarter

Study 4.4
LH Half - RH Eights

Study 4.5
LH Half - RH Sixteenths

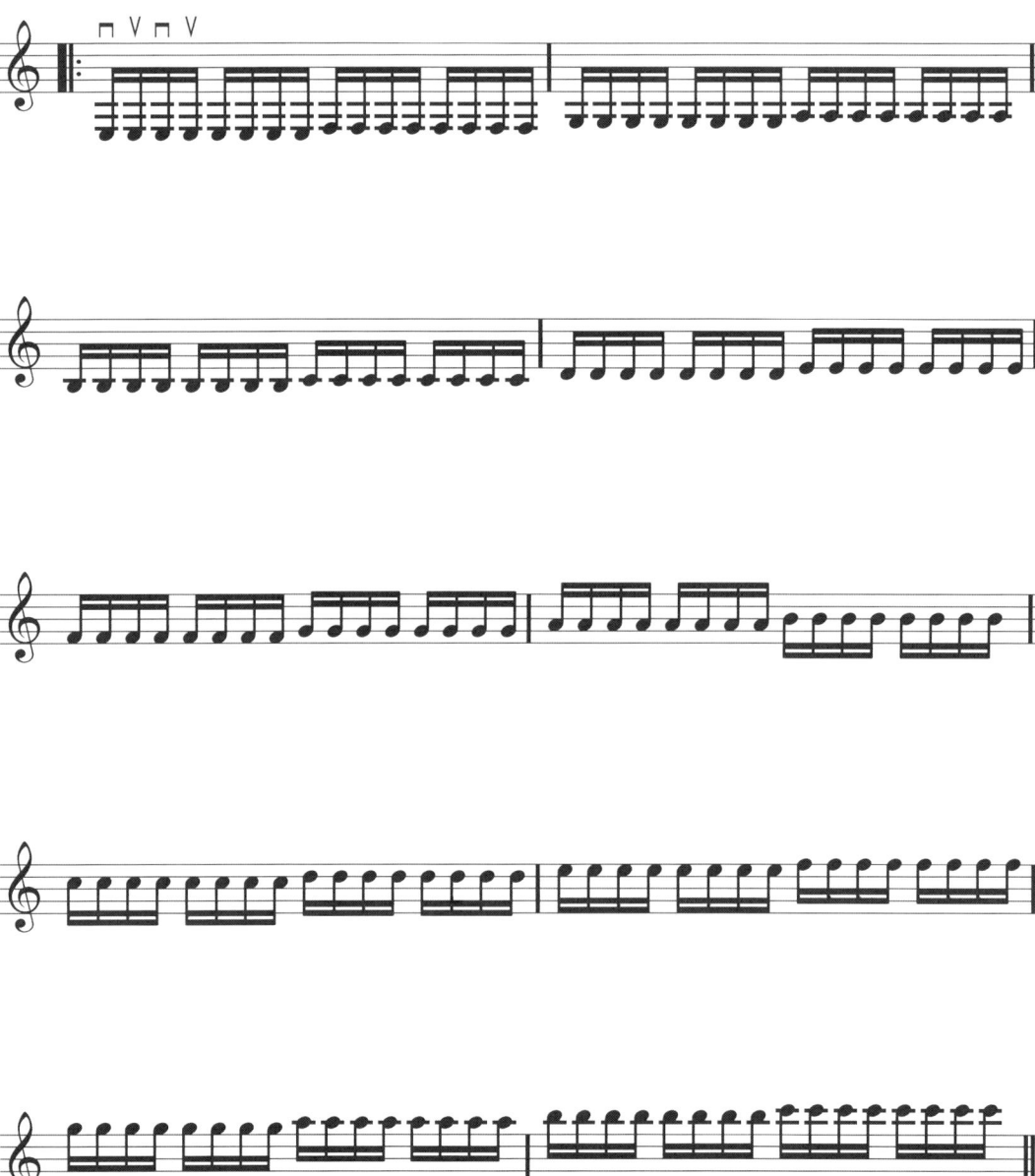

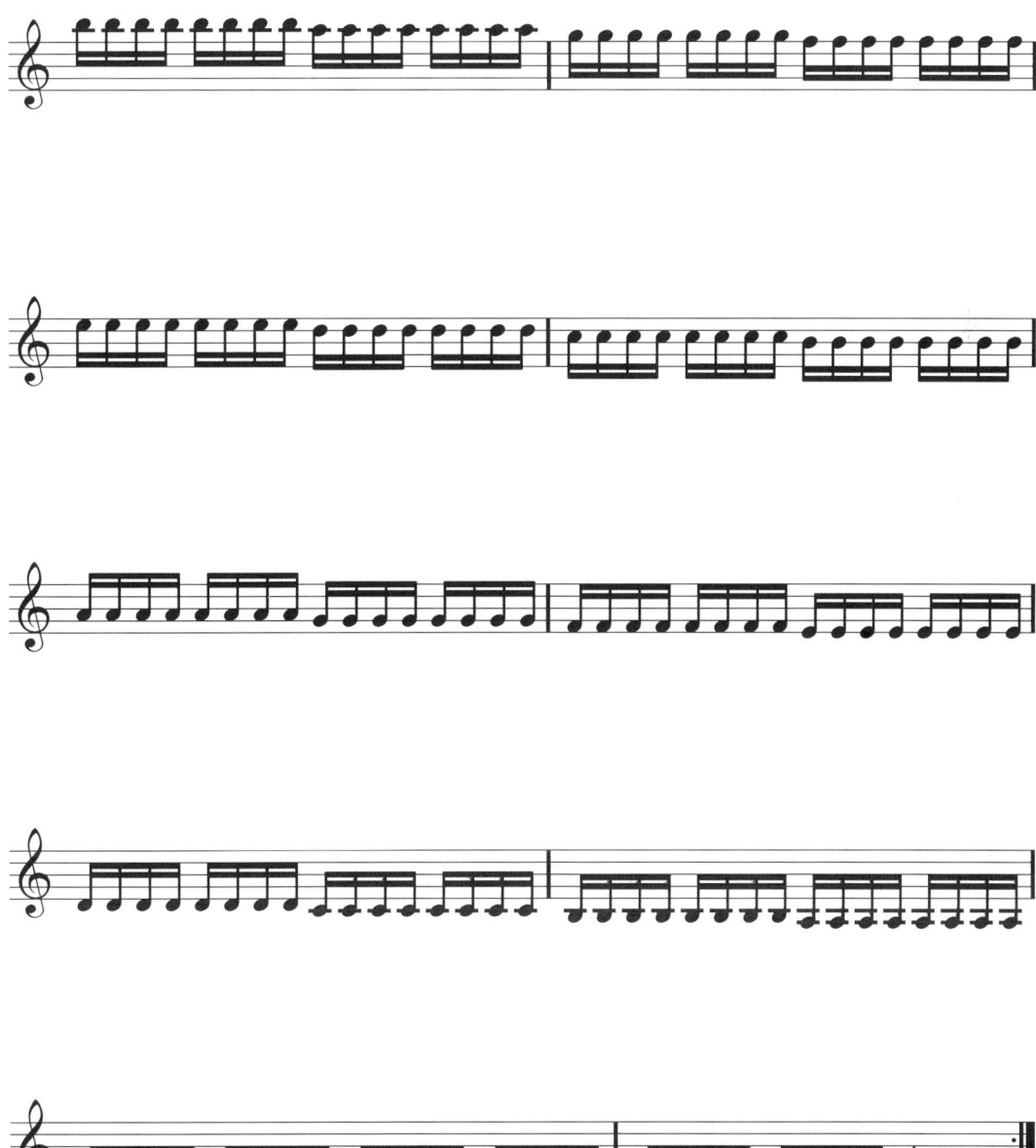

Study 4.6
LH Quarter - RH Quarter

Study 4.7
LH Quarter - RH Eights

Study 4.8
LH Quarter - RH Sixteenths

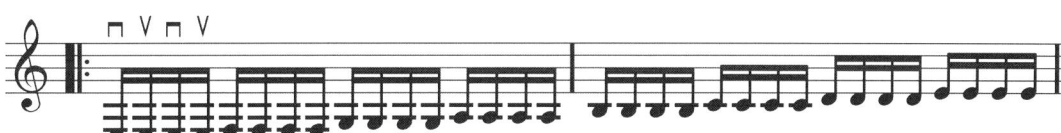

Study 4.9
LH Eights - RH Eights

Study 4.10
LH Eights - RH Sixteenths

Study 4.11
LH Sixteenths - RH Sixteenths

Study 4.12
Speed Study

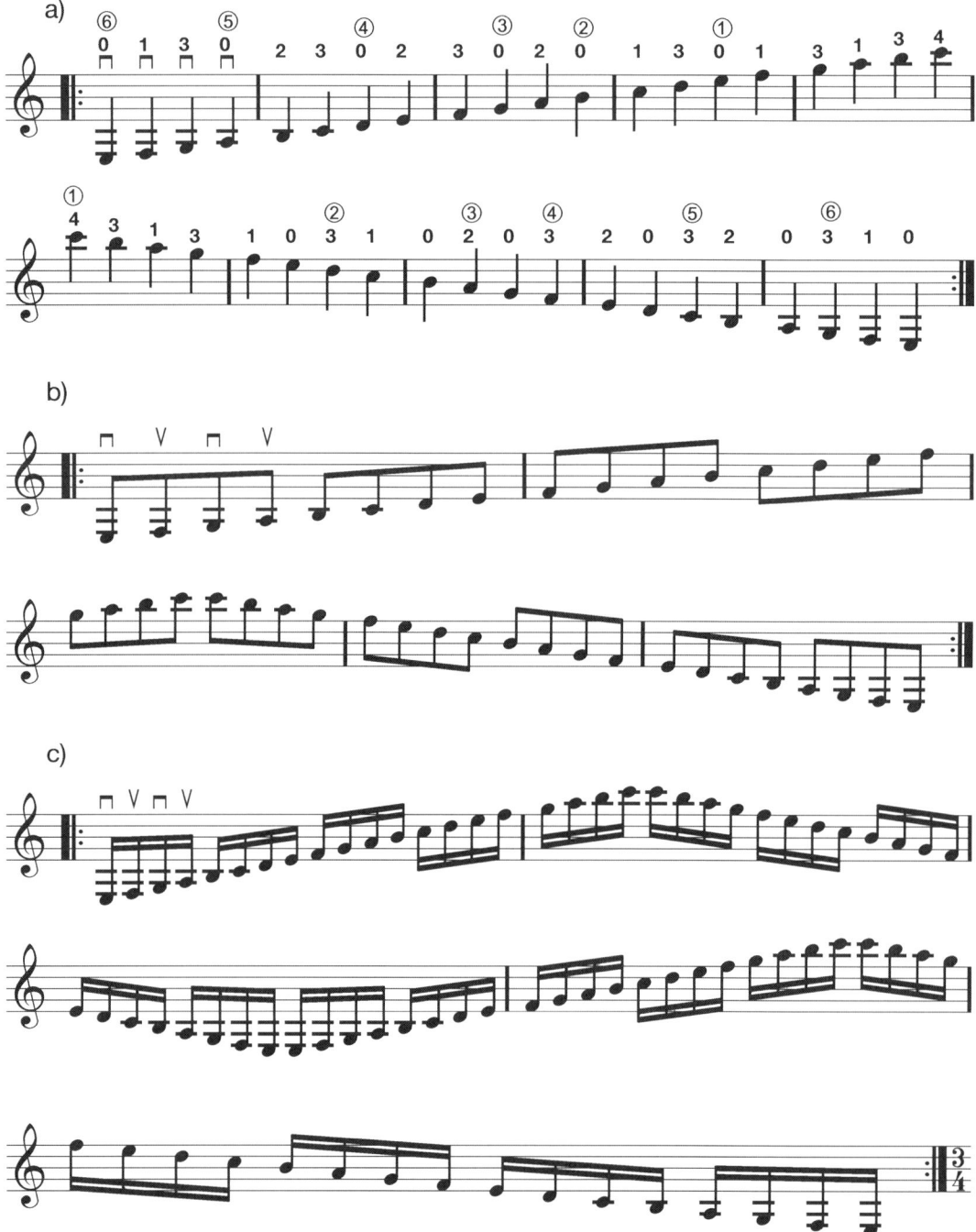

Study 4.13
Groups of Three

59

Study 4.14
Groups of Four

CHROMATIC SCALE

Study 4.16
Speed Study

Phrase as 5 note groups on each string and 4 note group on the 2nd string to ease learning.

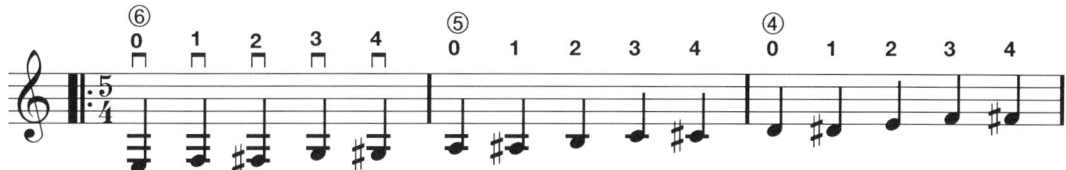

ABOUT MUSIC

There are four areas of music which will need to be conquered:

1) *The physical aspect* of playing your instrument.
2) *Counting* in time with in the rhythmic subdivisons.
3) *Note memorization* in relation to scale, fingering and related chord.
4) *Solfege Training* and the ability to transcribe pitch from mind to instrument.

This does not occur all at once but over a period of time, drop by drop.
Proceed in this order and it will eventually come to pass.

Chapter 5

E Minor Pentatonic Studies

E Blues Studies

*Either write things worth reading
or do things worth writing.*

Benjamin Franklin

E MINOR PENTATONIC

65

The majority of hammer-ons, pull-offs and basic licks built around the open-position chords are derived from this scale. It works well over the G, C, D, E Emin, A and Amin chords. Emaj and Amaj will give it a bluesy kind of sound.

REMEMBER:
Use a forward/downward pressure on the thumb towards the upper middle of the back of the neck. This allows the fingers to release freely like the hammers of a piano as the fingers strike the string. Use the fingers to tap the strings. Strive for machine like accuracy.

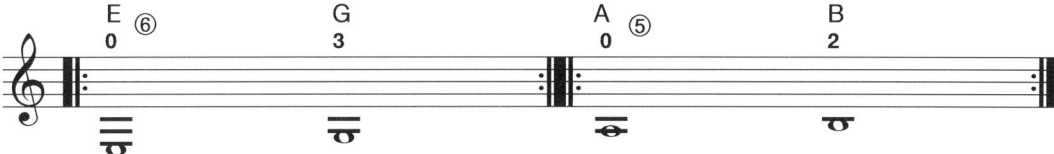

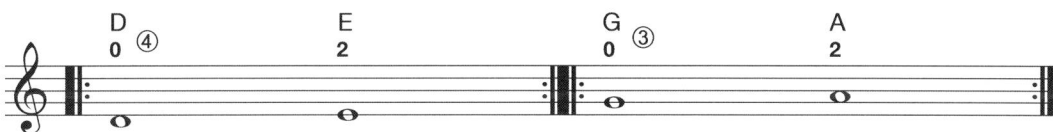

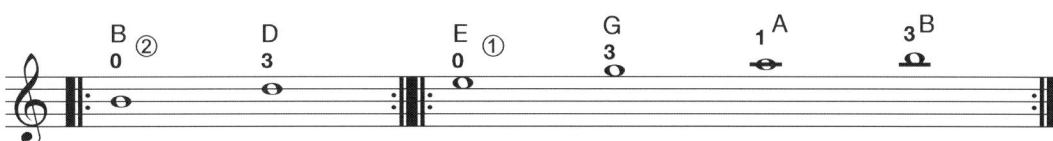

Study 5.1

Play slowly and evenly with a metronome.

REMEMBER:
down stroke - strike pick over the top of string into the next string below.
up stroke - strike pick over the top of string into the next string above.
down-up stroke - keep the pick as close to the center of string as possible.

Study 5.2
Speed Study

Study 5.3
Groups of Two

Study 5.4
Groups of Three

Study 5.5
Groups of Four

E BLUES SCALE

This particular blues scale is one of the most widely used for blues and pop. It has a nice gritty sound against the Emaj-Emin, Amaj-Amin, Gmaj and Cmaj open-position chords. There are also many articulation options through the use of hammer-ons, pull-offs and open string glides.

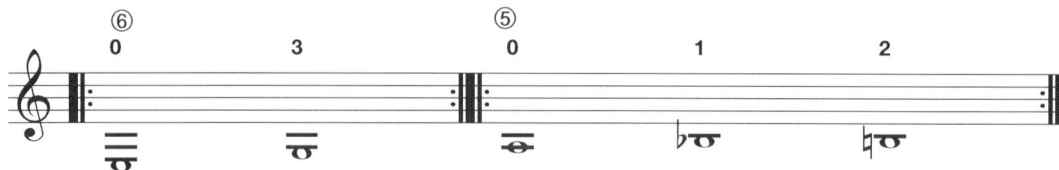

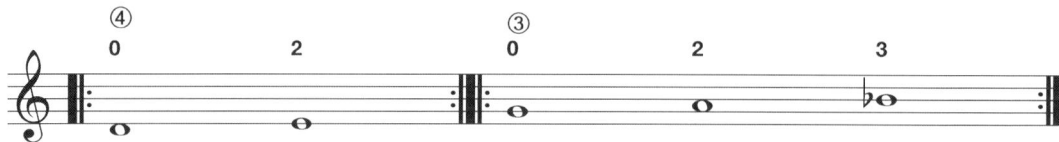

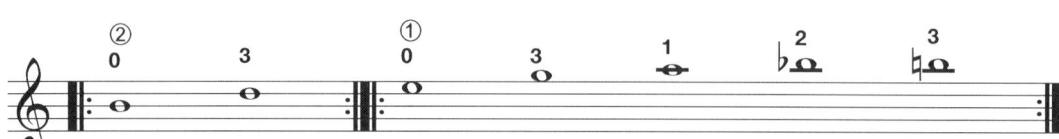

Study 5.7

Let each note ring to its full value.

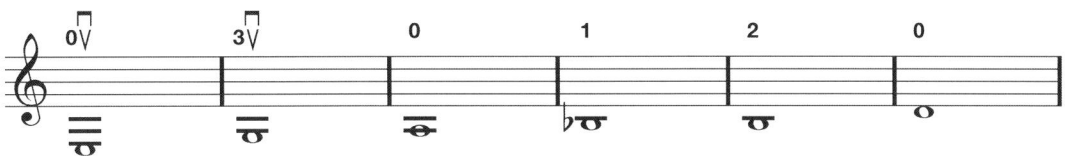

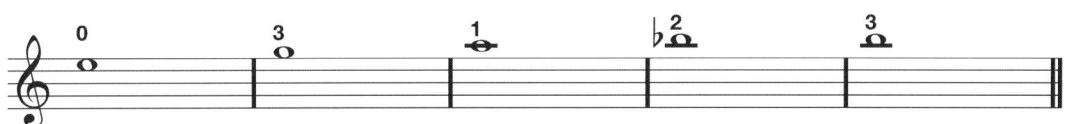
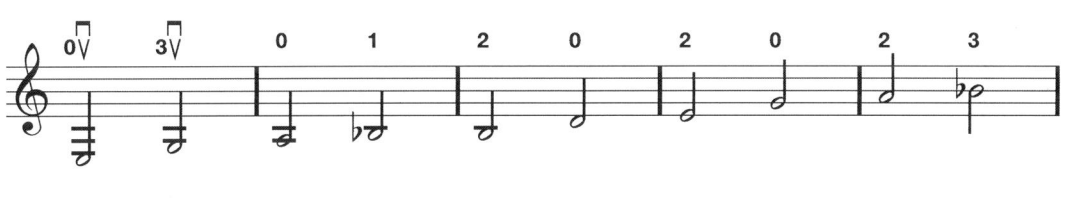
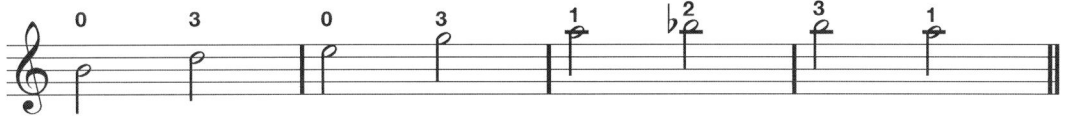

Study 5.8
Speed Study

Study 5.9
Groups of 3

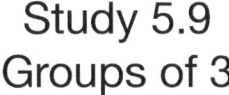

Study 5.10
Groups of 4

E Blues Study

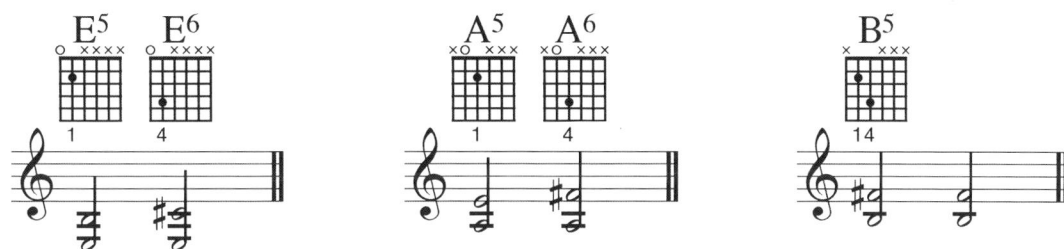

Study 5.11
12 Bar Blues

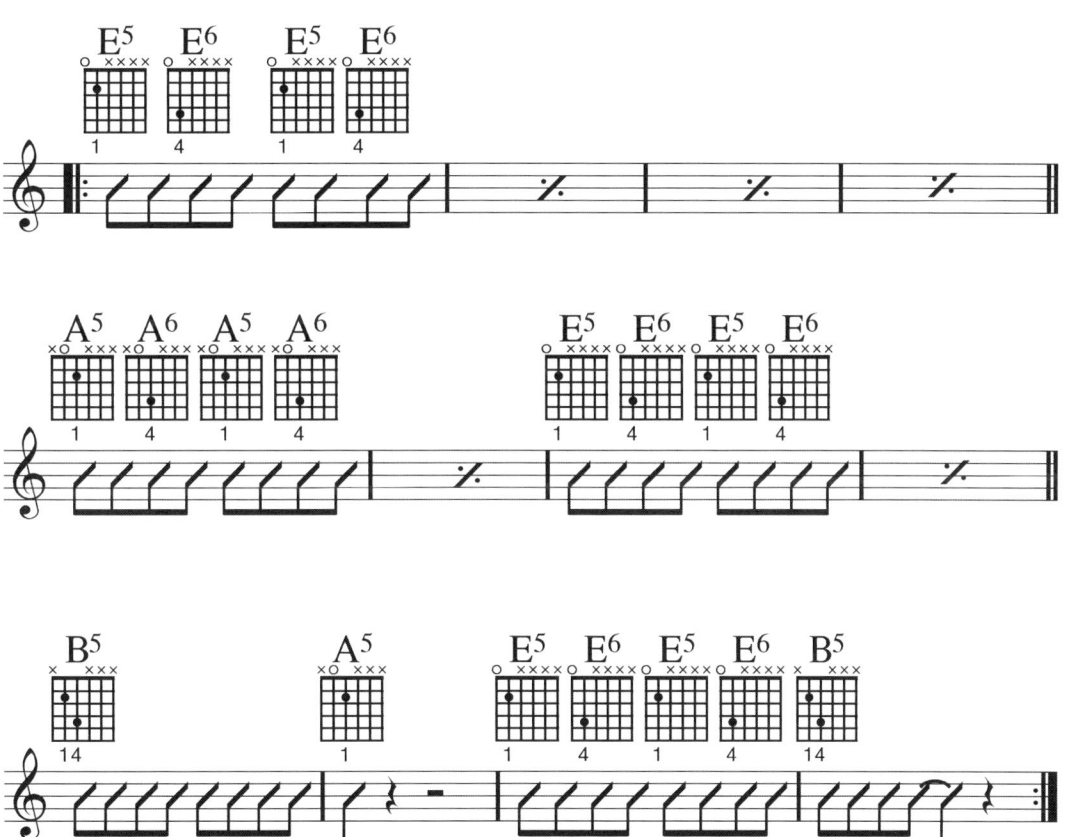

Study 5.12
2 measure lick

Study 5.13
2 measure phrases

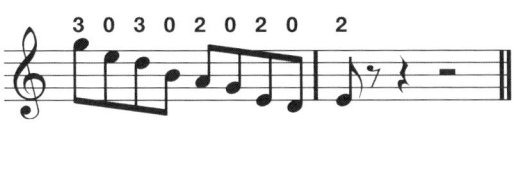

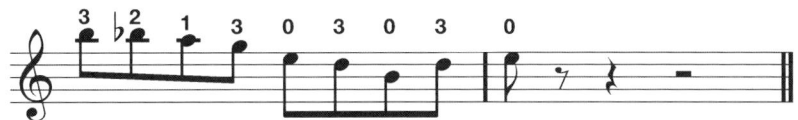

PART THREE

Chordal Studies

CHAPTER 6

Chords

I would advise you to keep your overhead down, avoid a major drug habit, play everyday and take it in front of other people.

They need to hear it and you need them to hear it.

- James Taylor -

Regular Review is Essential!

POWER CHORDS

Power Chords are the quickest way in to learning tunes. The fingers remain the same on the root and 5th of the chord. Another name for power chord is diads, two note chords. Power derives its name from the sound produced with tube distortion. In more advanced playing these structures open a world chordal sounds for composition.

Practice: 1) Play all the practice tunes with power chords. 2) Play chord workouts with power chords. 3) Take down one tune a day using power chords.

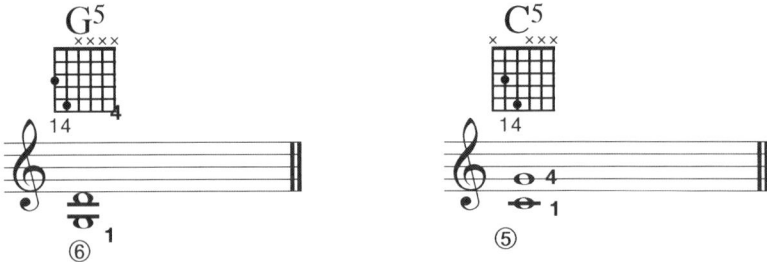

Root on 6th String

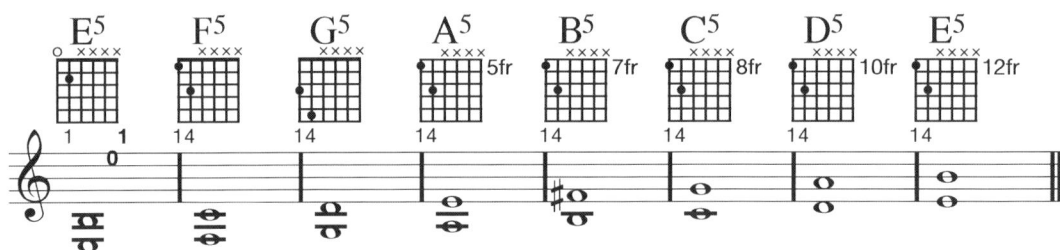

Root on 5th String

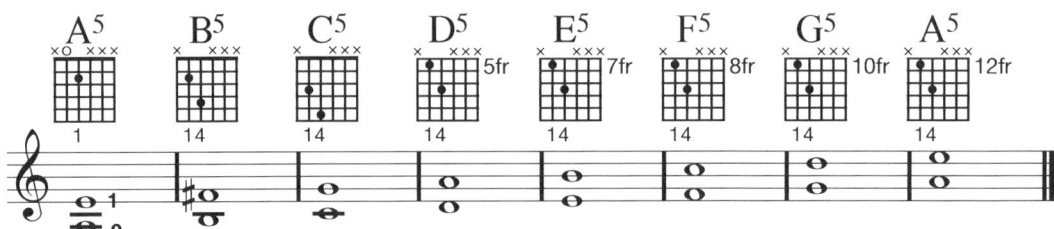

Study 6.1
Horizontal Movement

Root on 6th String

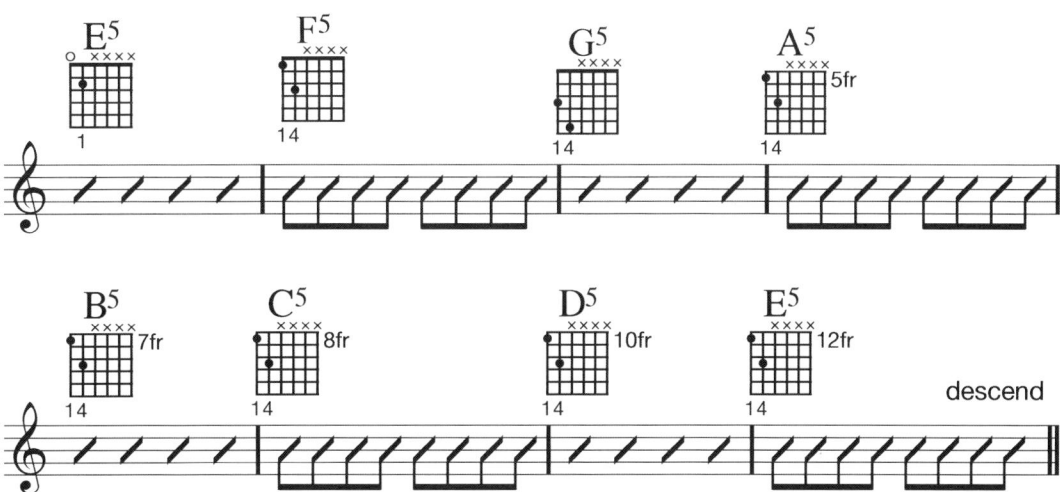

Root on 5th String

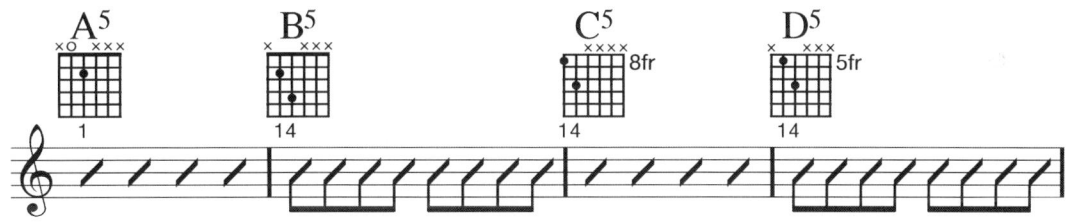

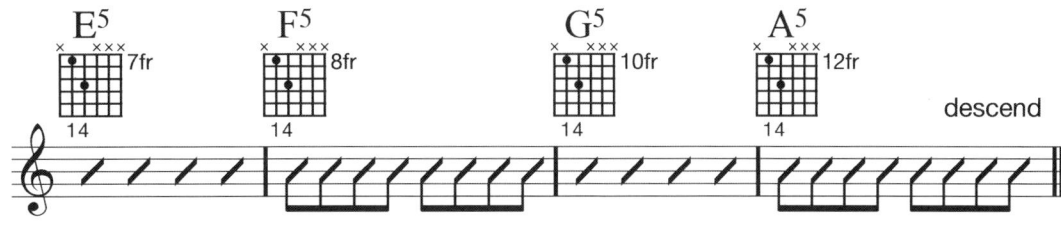

Study 6.2
Vertical Movement

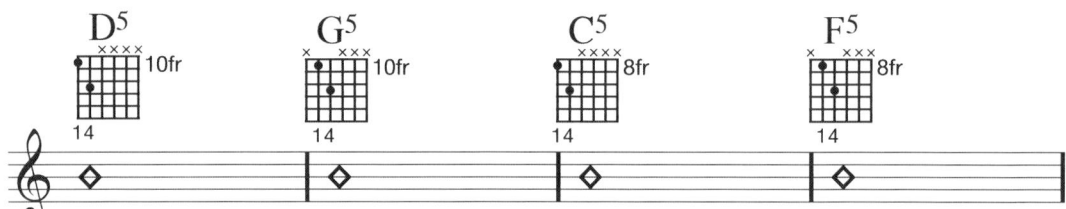

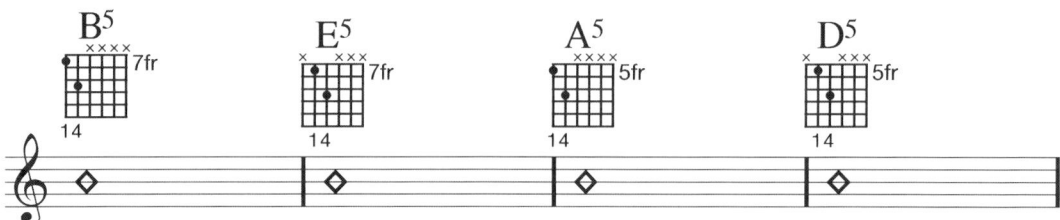

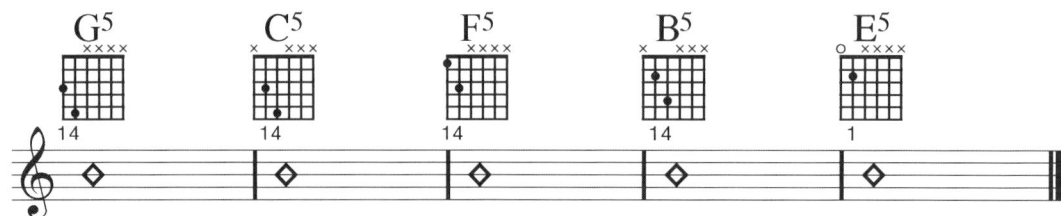

EIGHT OPEN-POSITION CHORDS

Study 6.3
Vertical Alignment

These are probably the most important chords in popular guitar music and certainly the set of chords from which all scales and related chords are derived from in this book.

Fingerings given use common finger movement. These fingerings allow the easiest transition between chords with a minimum of movement.

This grouping gives you six major chords and two minor chords. They shift vertically across the 6, 5 & 4 string groupings practiced in chapter 2.

GROUP 1

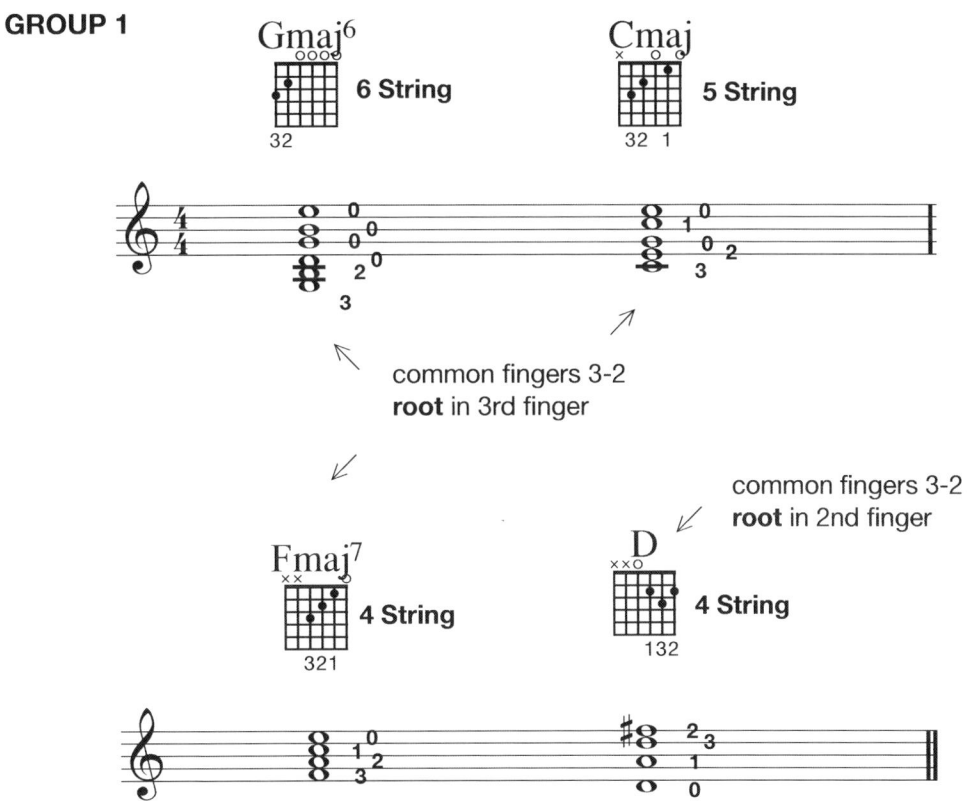

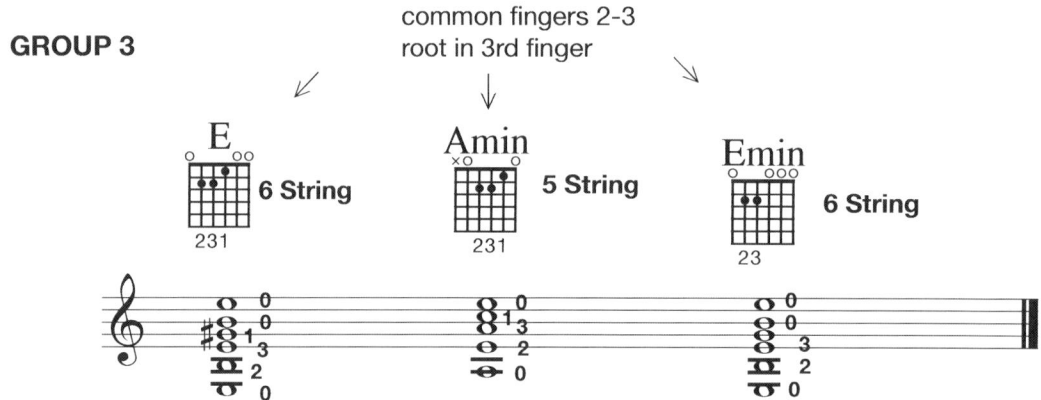

CHORD TRANSITION FORMULA

Study 6.4
New Shapes

a) **PRESS** and release chord shape on neck 16 times keeping fingers on strings.

b) **TAP** on neck with chord shape 16 times lifting fingers 1/8 inch off strings while holding shape.

c) **SCATTER** fingers and shape 8 times. Lift fingers off strings and lose shape. Very accurately return to shape.

d) Repeat until shape is memorized in hands and can accurately and easily return to finger placement every time.

Study 6.5
Chord Transition

a) **TRACK** - Track RH pick and LH finger movements by touching lowest note string of each LH chord with pick only, no strumming.

b) **MARK** - Focus only on accuracy - no time is used. Only accurate LH finger movement and RH string grouping. Notice any similarities between shapes and use mind over fingers to help them learn the movement.

c) **PLAY TIME** - With the L.H. holding each chord 4 pulses per measure, the R.H. subdivides using first whole, 1/2, and then 1/4 notes strikes. This means the chord movement shifts from to 3 pulses, 1 pulse, 1/8 pulse respectively.

Speed always comes with accurate movement first. These exercises force accuracy in order to build speed. Always work with a metronome.

STUDY 6.6
Chord Transition Example

Mark:
focus on movement acuracy only
no tempo

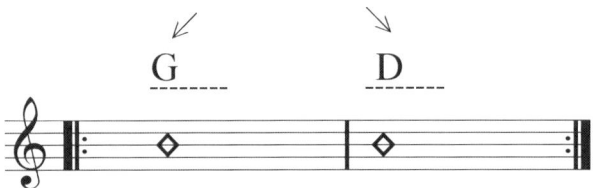

a) Left Hand moves within 4 counts. PLAY IN TIME.

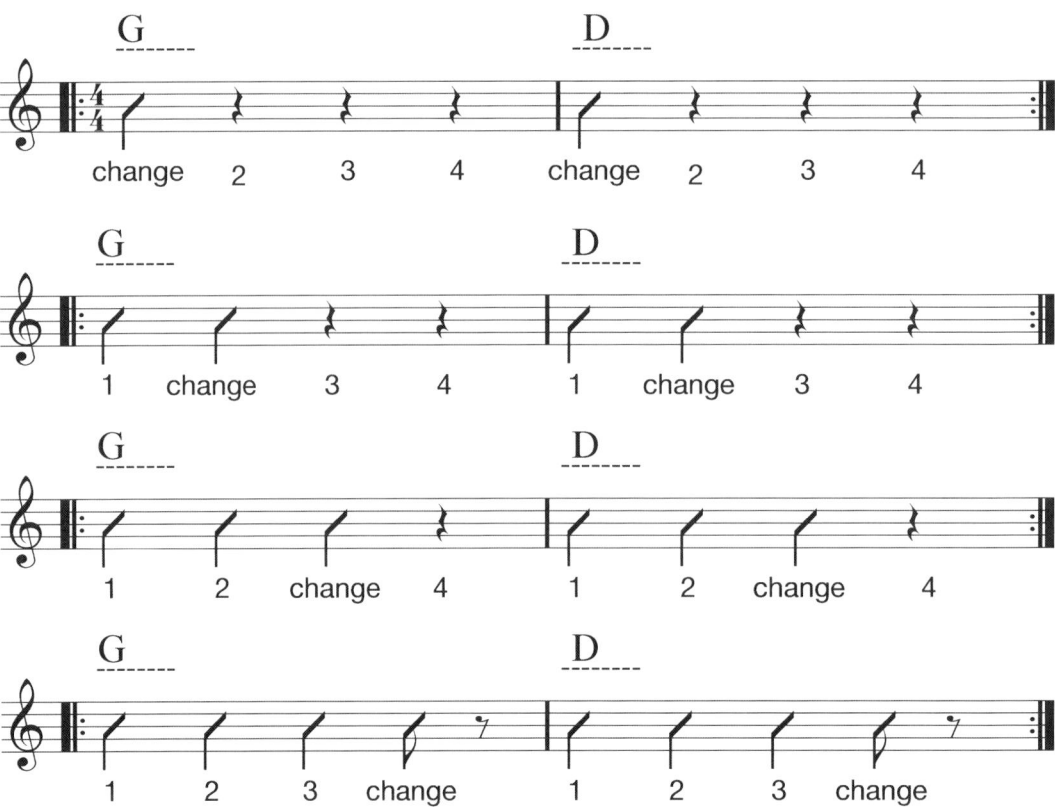

b) Left hand moves within 2 counts.

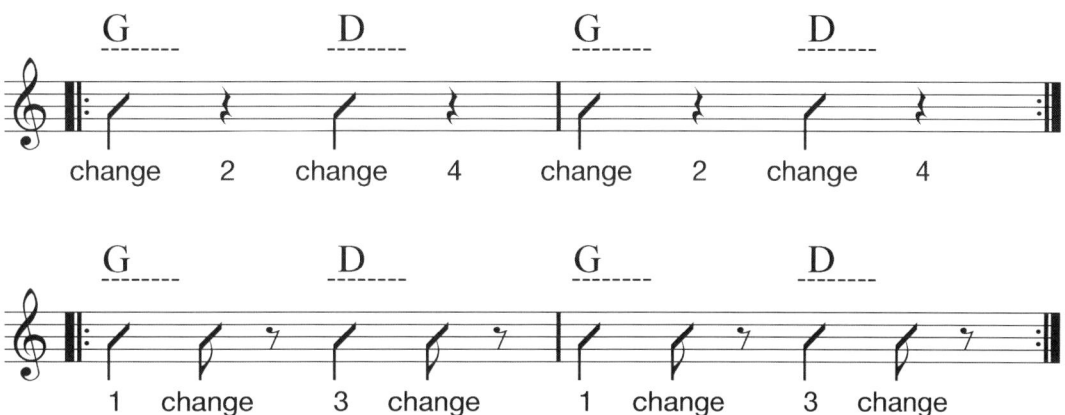

At this point you can handle 80% of any two chord shifts you are working on.

c) Left hand moves every count.

By this time you will be able to handle most any situation which requires the chord movement you have been working on.

Study 6.7
Six Major Chords

These major cords derived from the Eight open-chords constitute the majority of your basic pop tunes on guitar. I view them as only three interrelated shapes for quick memory and ease of learning.

Third finger carries the chord name. Amaj is the exception, root found in first finger.

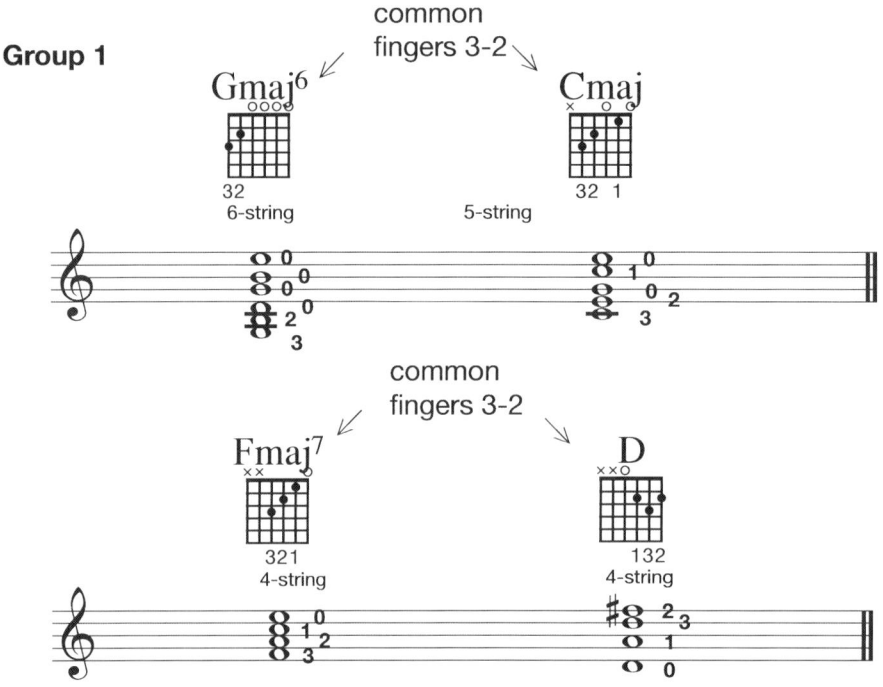

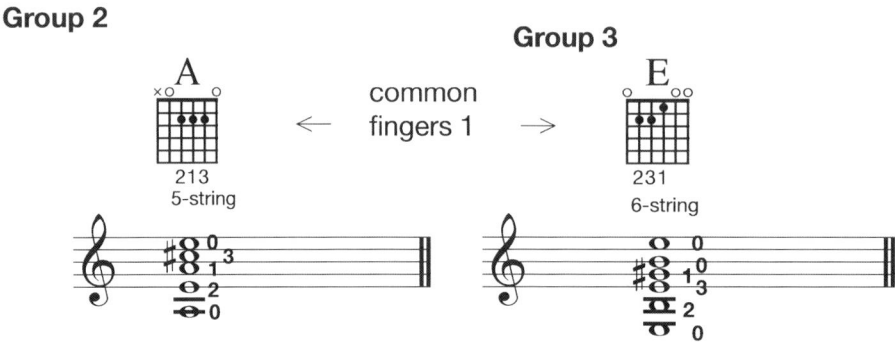

Study 6.8
Horizontal Movement

89

This is another way of cementing the eight shapes into your left hand while the right hand learns the proper string grouping. It also creates some nice sounds.

Practice using the movement formula.

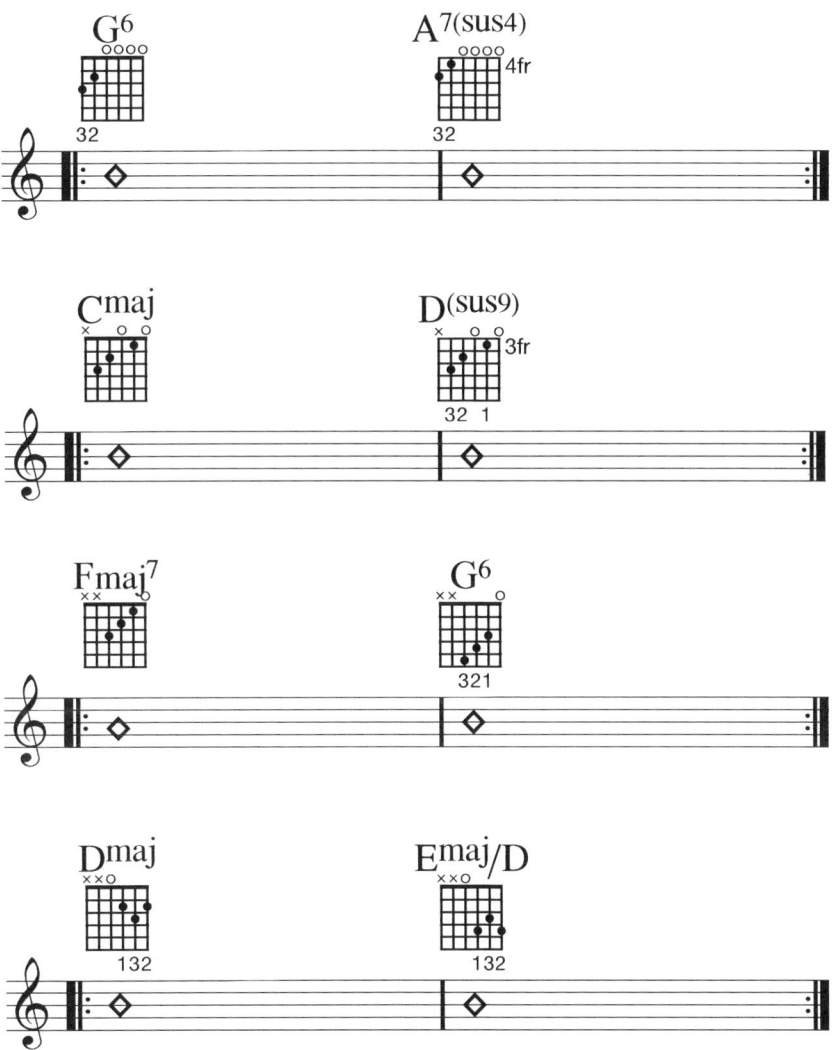

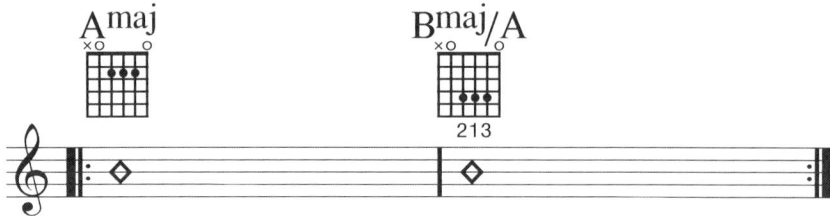
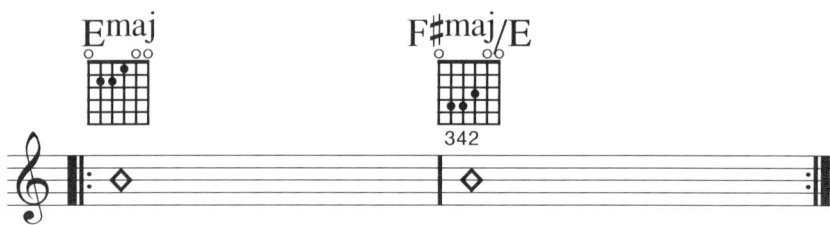
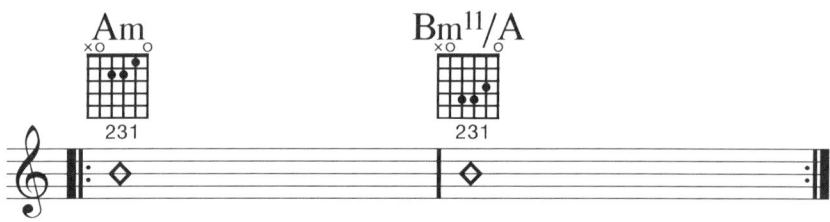
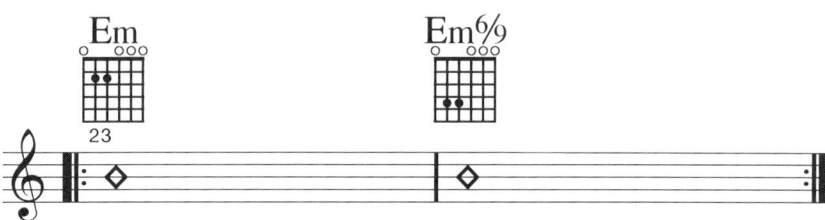

PRACTICE PROGRESSIONS #1

91

This sequencing of the 8 open-position chords will help to embed the movement and finger relationships into your left hand and the 6, 5, 4 grouped string relationships into the right hand.

If you have trouble moving between chords see the Chord Transition Formulas on pages 85-86.

1)

2)

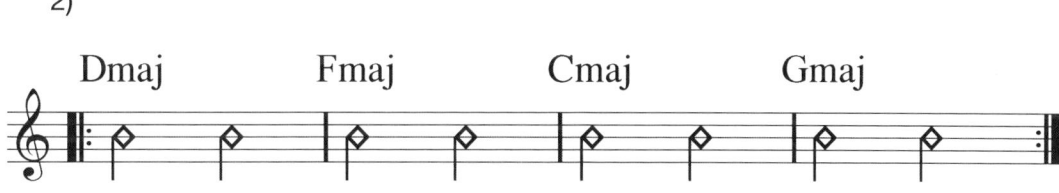

3)

4)

5)
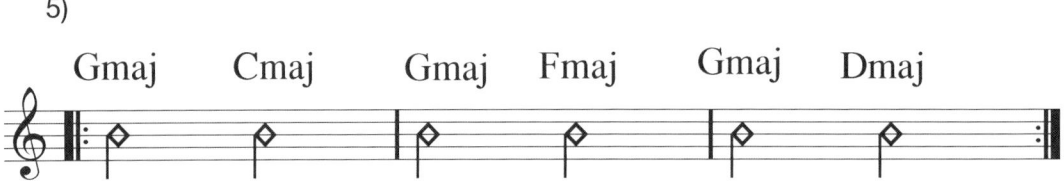

6)
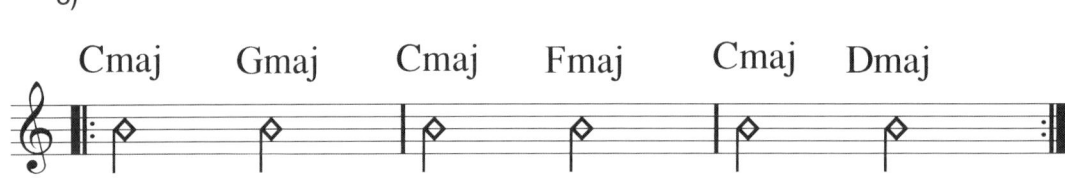

7)
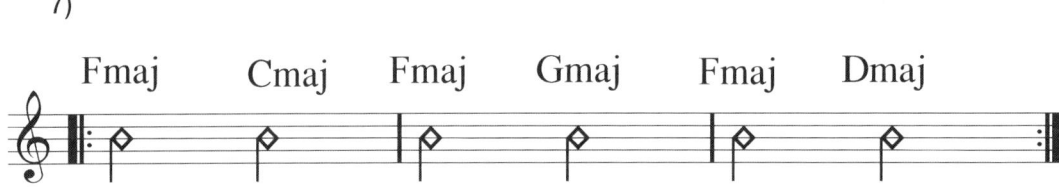

8)
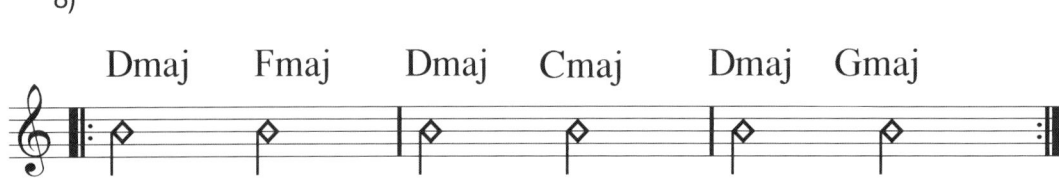

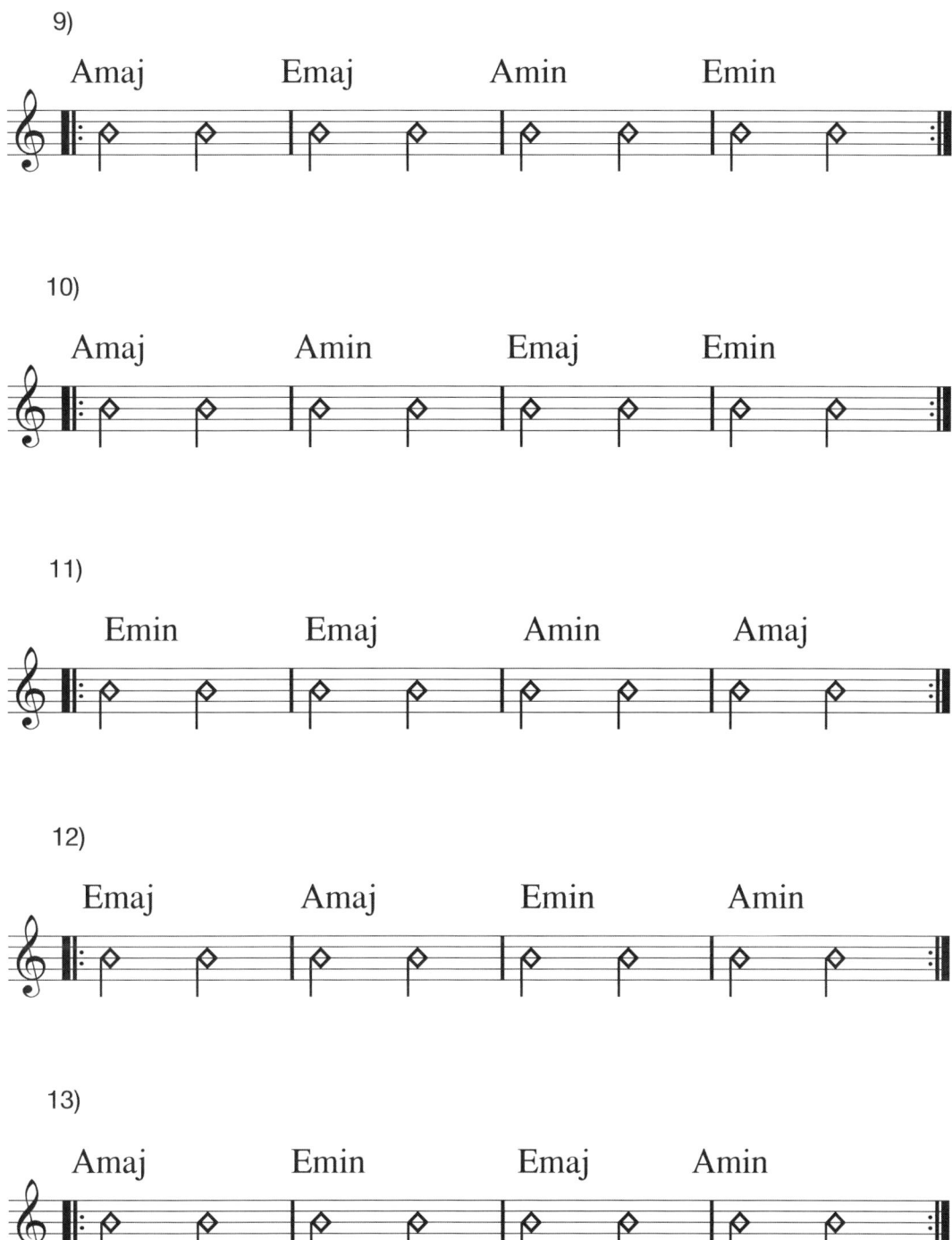

14)

15)

16)
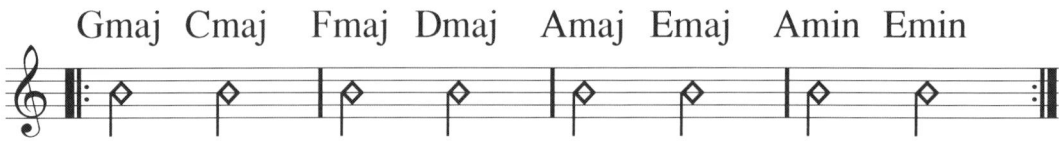

17)
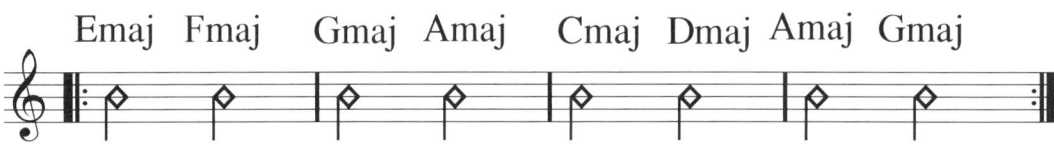

RHYTHM GUITAR #3

Folk Strum Patterns 1

When learning right hand rhythms, first mute all strings with the left hand. This creates a percussive effect. Focus on right hand strumming only. When comfortable with the pattern, place it in the context of the chords.

BASIC

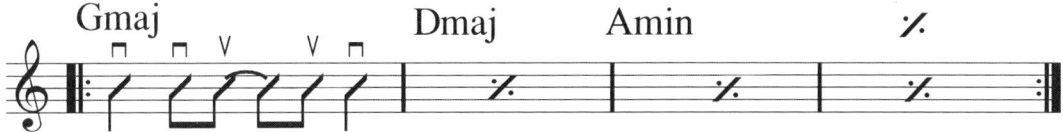

VARIATION #1

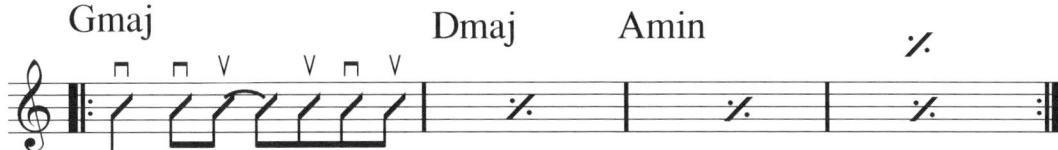

VARIATION #2

Study 6.9
Practice Song

Modern Chord Theory
Diatonic Triads

In the key of C major (CDEFGABC) if C is 1, then D is 2, E is 3, F is 4, G is 5, A is 6, B is 7. In Modern Chord Theory we use capitalized roman numerals to mark all major and minor chords; Imaj - IImin - IIImin - IVmaj - Vmaj - VImin - VIIdim.

In any given major key there are:

Three major chords
Imaj - IVmaj - Vmaj

Three minor chords
IImin - IIImin - VImin

One diminshed chord:
VIIdim (a special case minor chord called diminished).

These Chords occur as 3 note triads.

A **triad** is a chord with only three chord tones. These are the 1st, 3rd, and 5th notes of the chord. You can play a six string G major chord and still have only three notes in the chord. Triads are used mainly in rock, pop and blues.

Triads in any major key:
I - IV - V = major triads
II - III - VI = minor triads
VII = diminished

Triad Spelling
C major Triad is spelled:
1 - 3 - 5 or C - E - G

C minor triad is spelled:
1 - b3 - 5 or C - Eb - G

C diminished triad is spelled:
1 - b3 - b5 or C - Eb - Gb

MEMORIZE THESE FORMULAS:

Triads:
I major, II minor, III minor, IV major, V major, VI minor, VII diminished

Quiz Yourself:
The Key of G maj has how many sharps?

One sharp, F#.

Spell Scale:
G, A, B, C, D, E, F#

Name & Spell Triad Chords:
G maj, Amin, B min, Cmaj, D maj, E min, F# dim.

Using roman numeral analysis, it becomes very easy to transpose chord progressions into different keys. Here are some common formulas:

a) I - VI - II - V
b) II - V - I
c) III - VI - II - V - I
d) I - IV - V - IV - I

Can you transpose these formulas to the keys of:

G major:

C major:

F major:

D major:

A major:

E major:

PRACTICE PROGRESSIONS #2

99

These are very important chord progressions. They use the most common open string major chord combinations in their most available keys. They are found in much of the popular music written for guitar in the last 100 years. You will probably come across at least one of these combinations in any given tune.

I - IV - V PROGRESSIONS

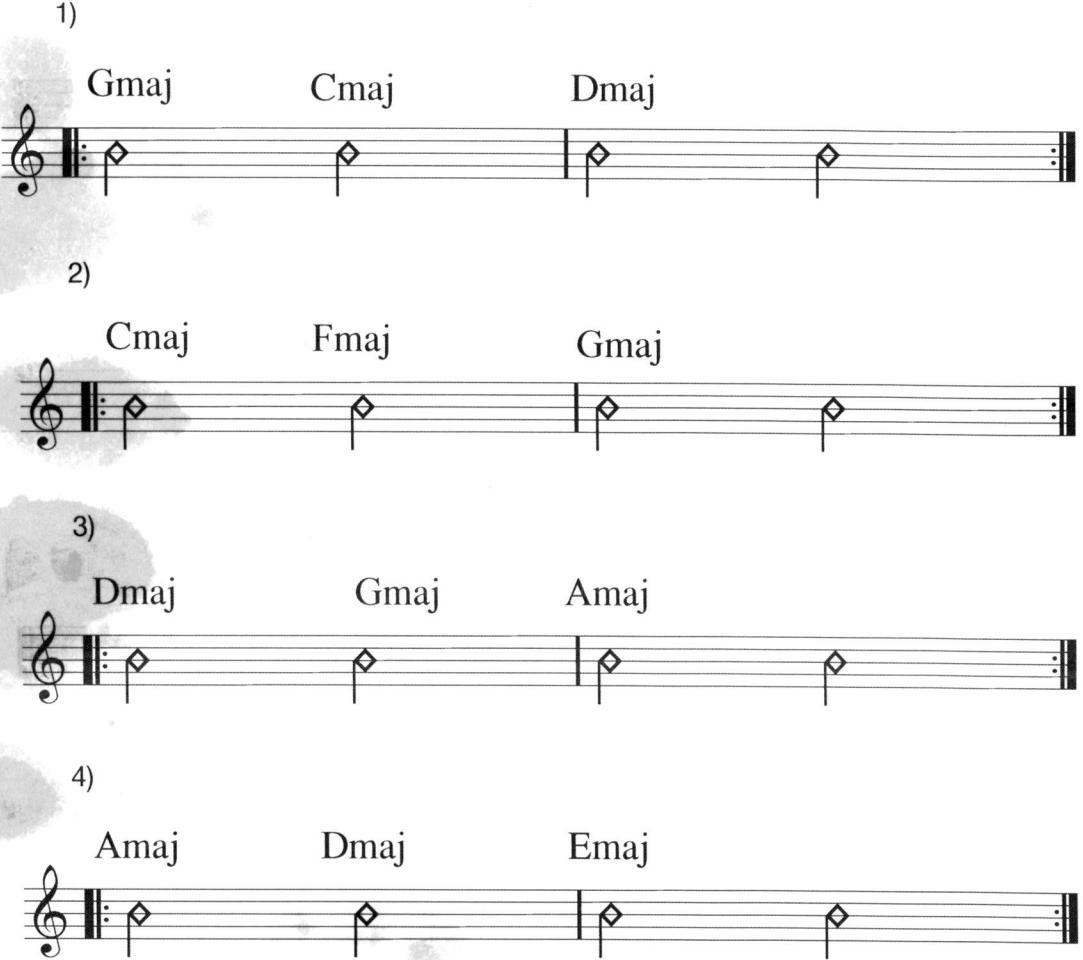

I - V PROGRESSIONS

I - IV - flat VII - IV PROGRESSIONS

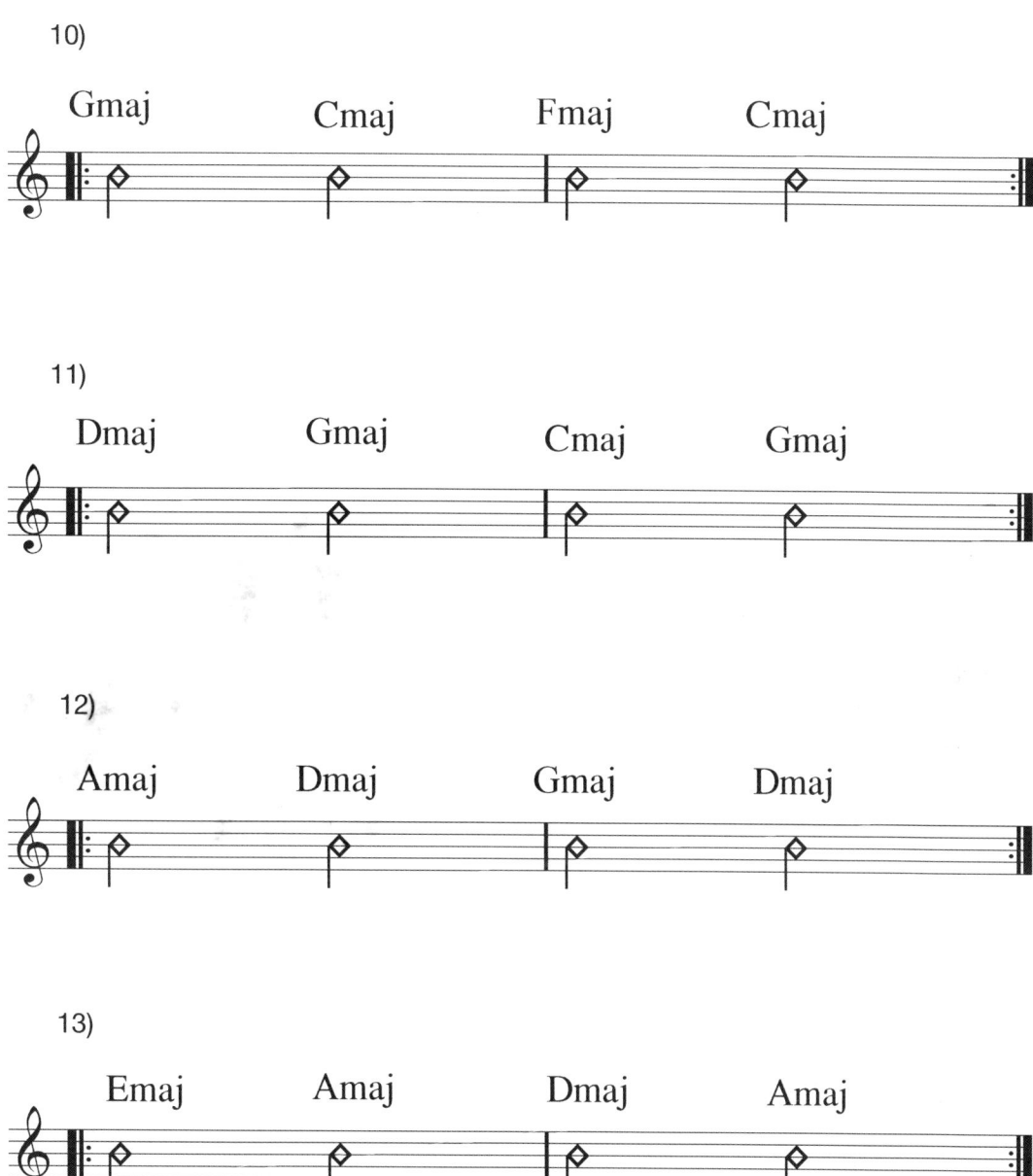

CHAPTER 7

Chords Part 2

Words have the power to destroy or heal. When they are both true and kind, they can change the world.

Buddha

RHYTHM GUITAR #4

ROCK BALLAD

BASIC

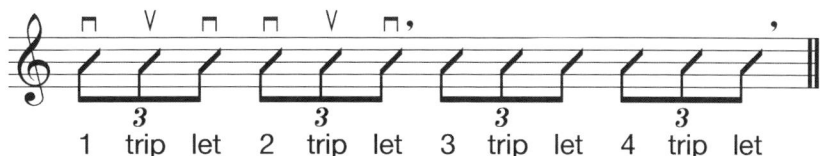

VARIATION

BASIC LATIN

BASIC

VARIATION

PRACTICE PROGRESSIONS #3

Common Chord Patterns

1)

I maj, VImin, IImin, V7

G, Emin, Amin, D

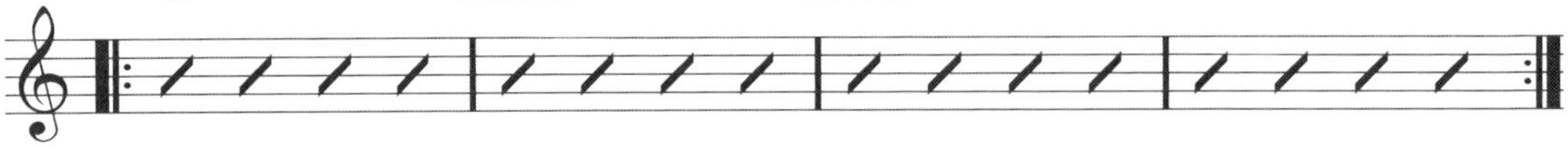

2)

IIImin

Bmin

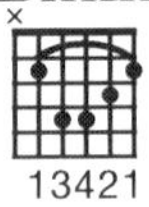

13421

VImin, IImin, V

Emin, Amin, D

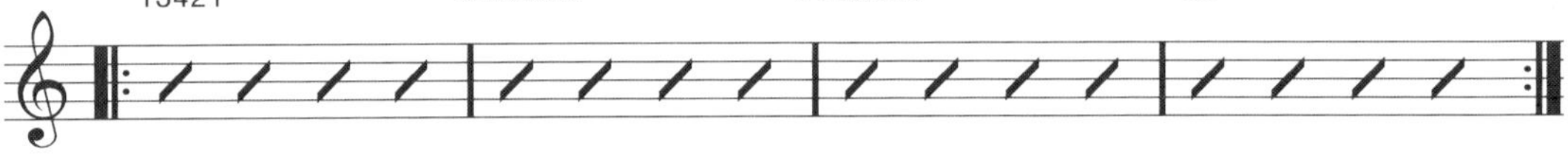

3)

Imaj, IImin, IVmaj, V

G, Amin, Cmaj, D

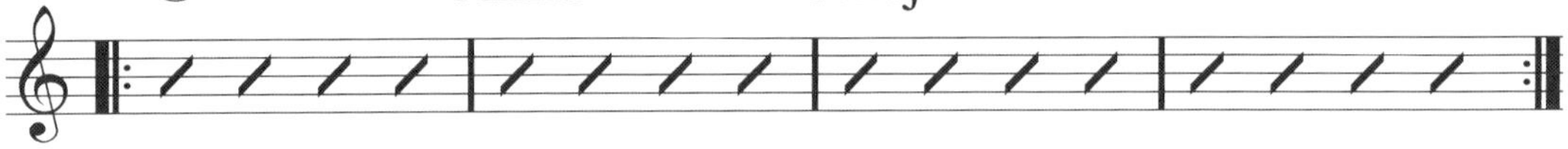

4)

VImin, Imaj, IImin7, IVmaj7

Emin, Gmaj, $Amin^7$, $Cmaj^7$

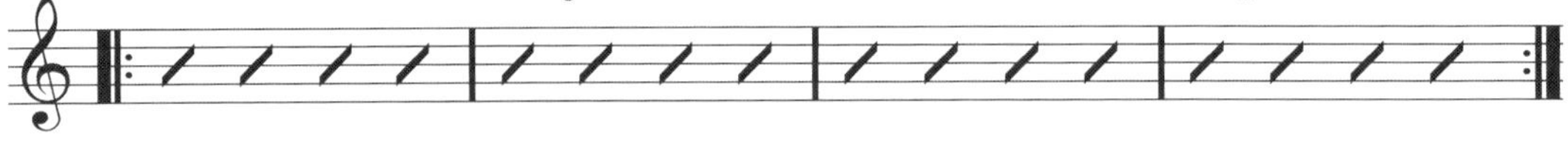

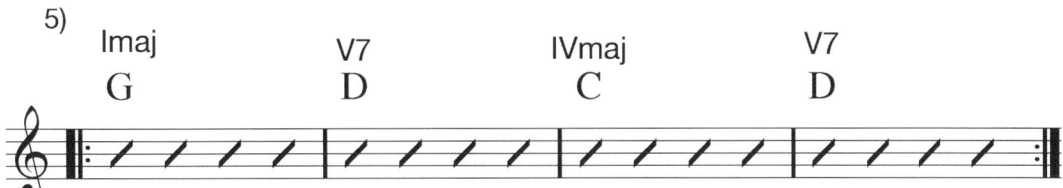
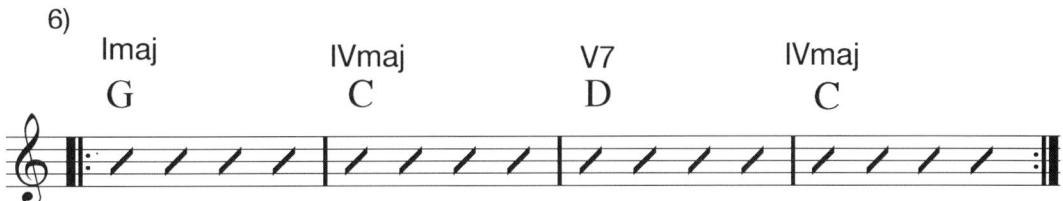

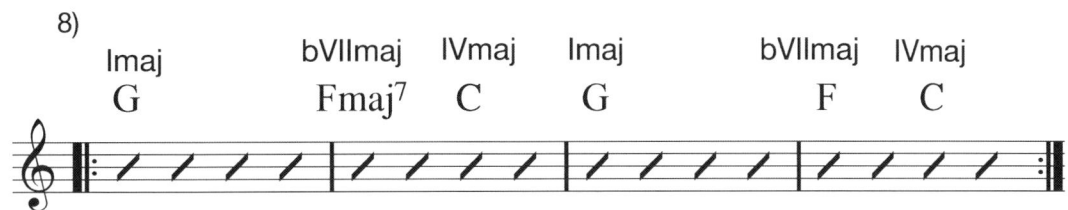

NINE OPEN POSITION CHORDS

This regrouping of the eight basic open position chords yields nine chords total. It focuses on chords with common right hand string groupings (6, 5 and 4). The D min chord is now added to give a total of nine open-string chords. G major now has the optional 4th finger added. F major now has an optional 1st finger mini barre added.

Study 7.1
Horizontal Alignment

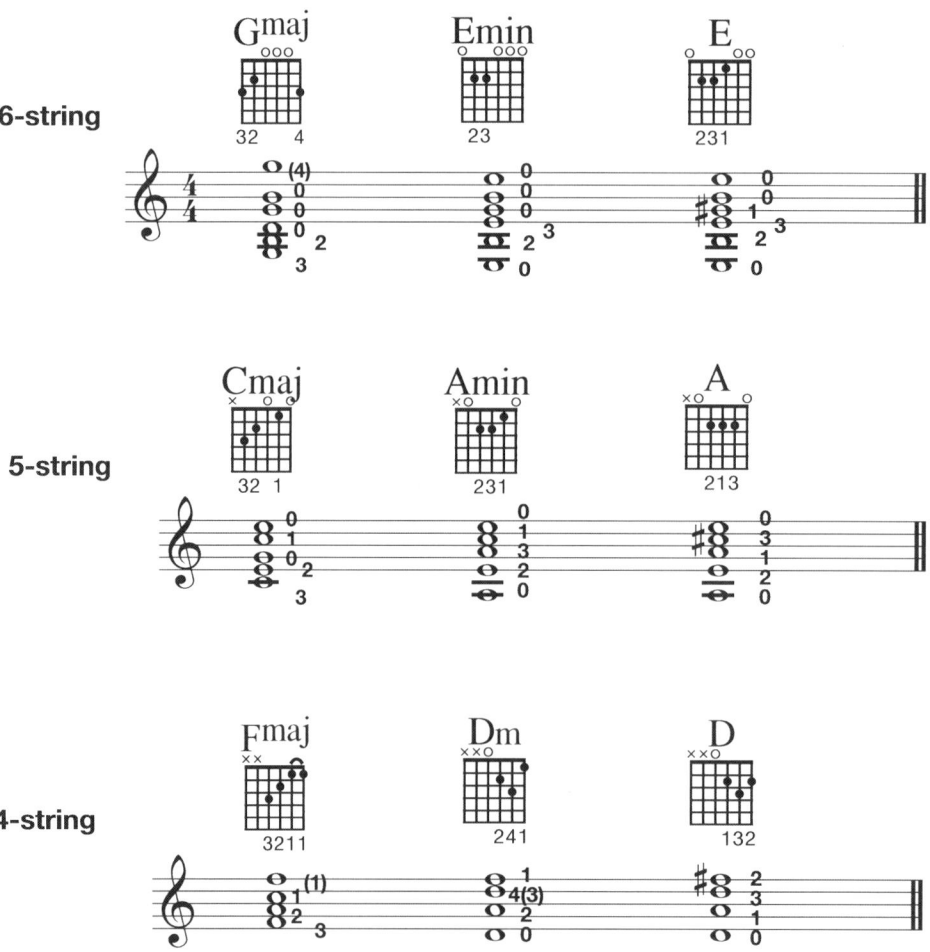

PRACTICE PROGRESSIONS #4

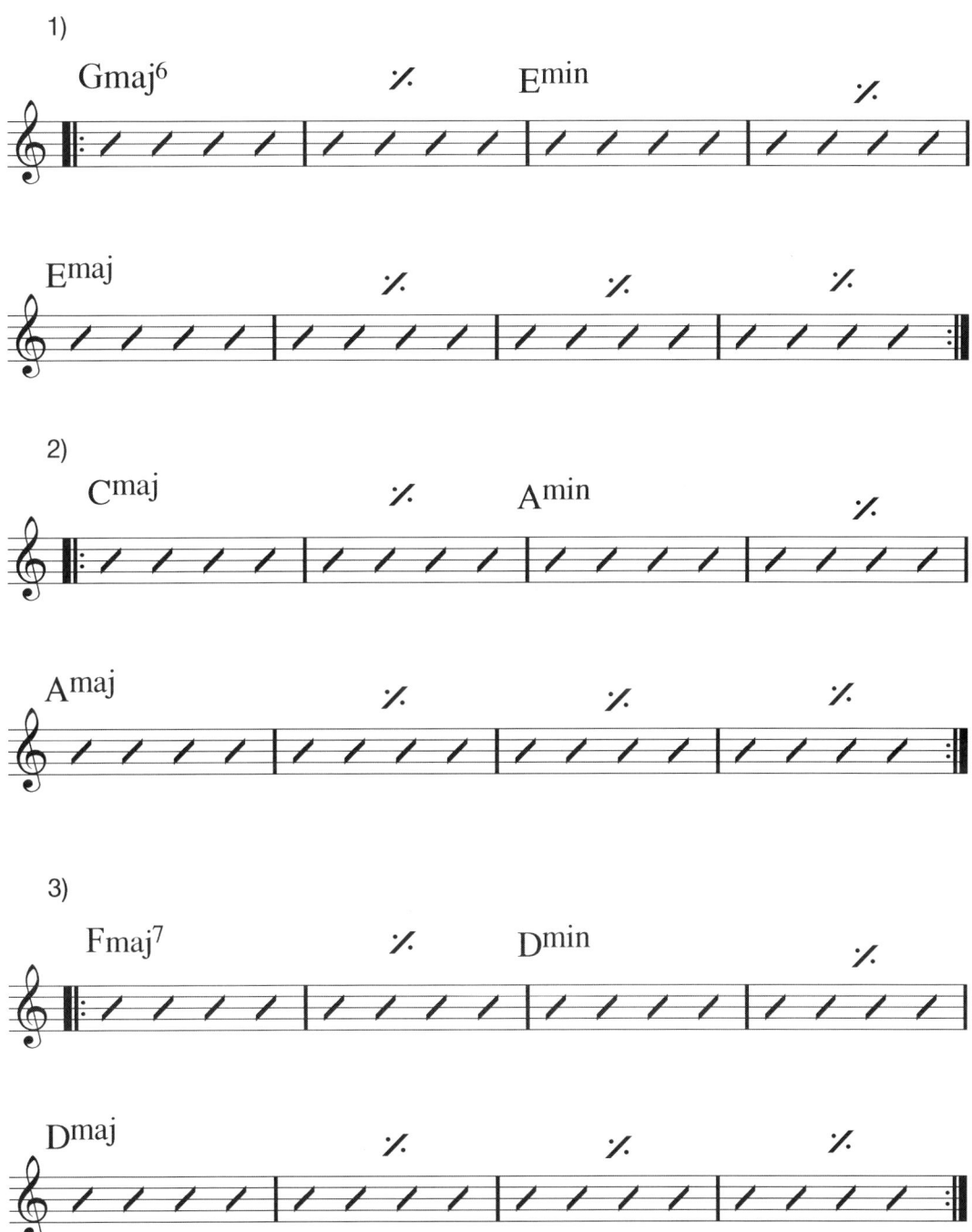

4)

5)

6)
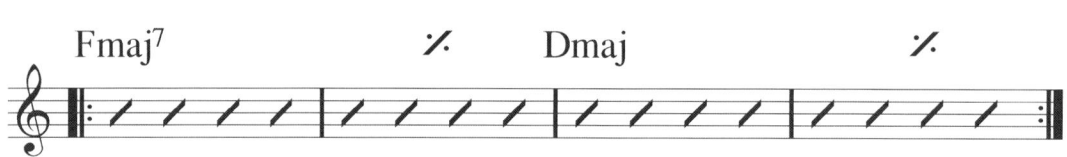

7)
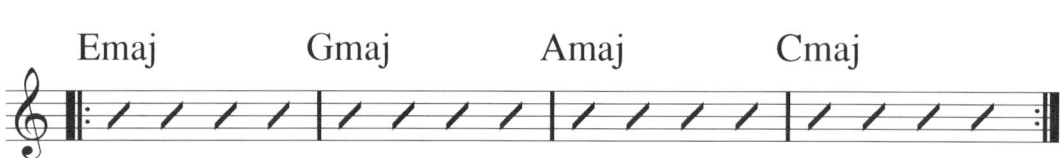

8)
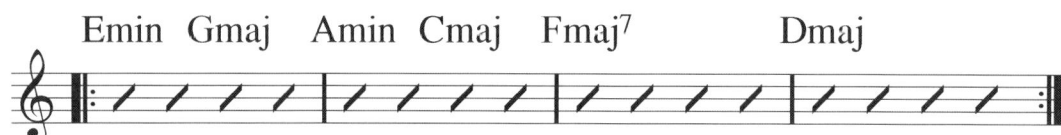

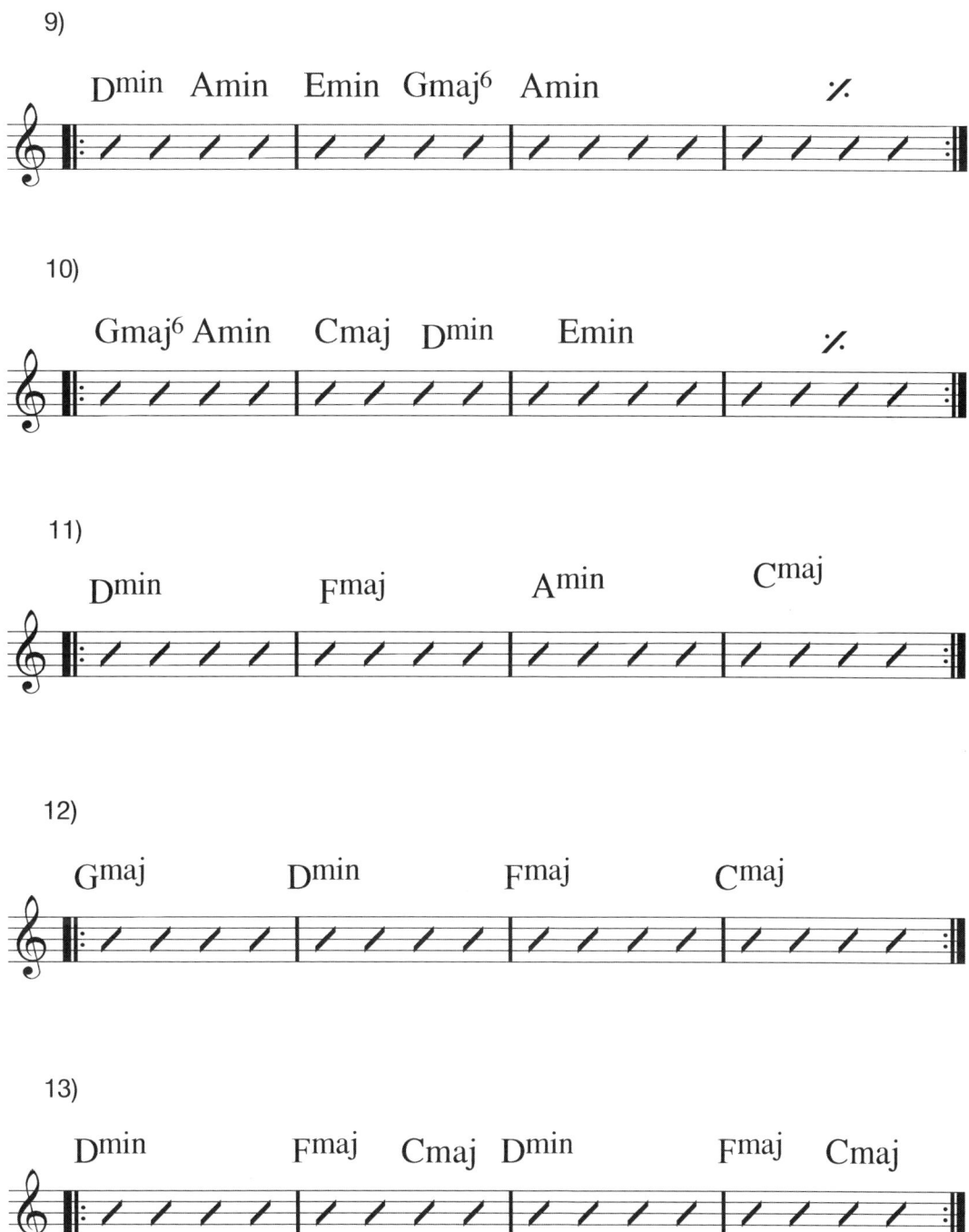

SPECIAL-CASE CHORDS

Study 7.2
Vertical Alignment

This is a very hip way to play the GCFDEA combinations. Interchange these chords if you want to add a bluegrass or contemporary sound to the tune you are playing.

a) common fingers
   2-1-3-4

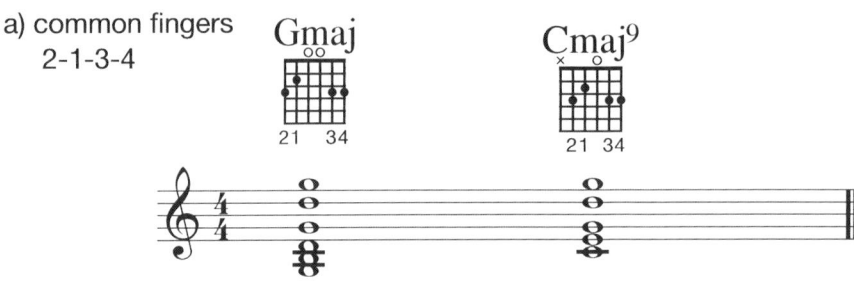

b) common fingers
   2-1-3-4

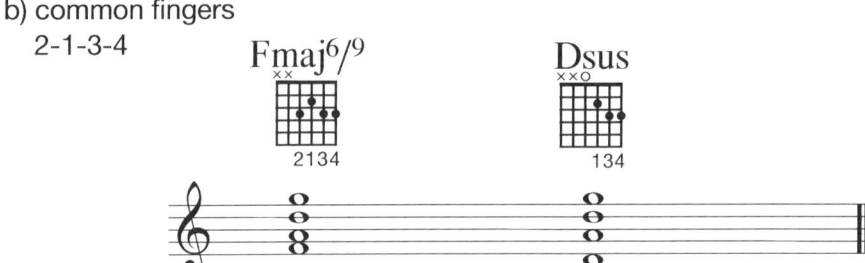

c) common fingers
   1-2-3-4

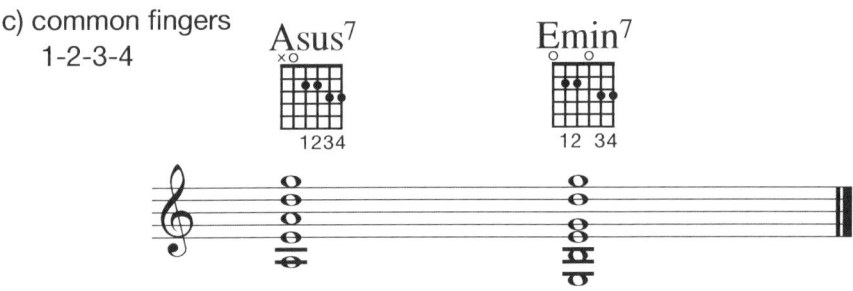

RHYTHM GUITAR #5

Boom - Chick Rhythm

Standard guitar strum pattern used in open chord playing for folk, country, bluegrass. Think low high low high etc. The guitar is performing 2 functions: 1) bass (low) (boom) and 2) banjo (high) (chick).

BASIC

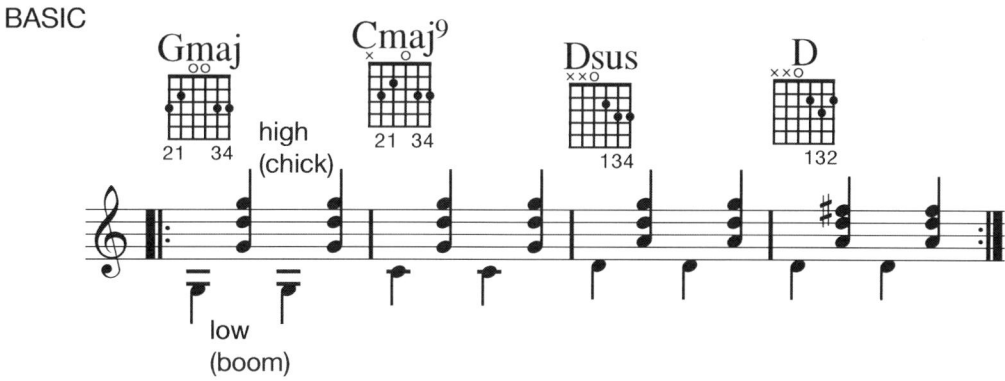

VARIATION

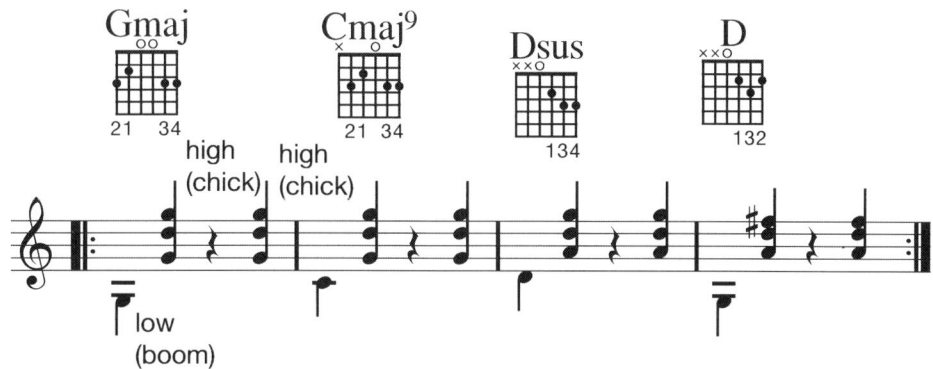

SPECIAL-CASE CHORDS

Study 7.3
Horizontal Alignment

6-string

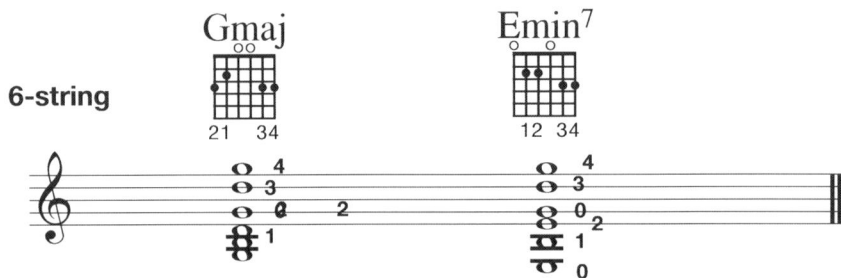

5-string

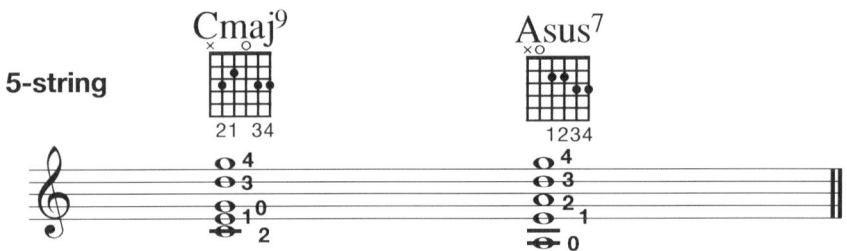

4-string

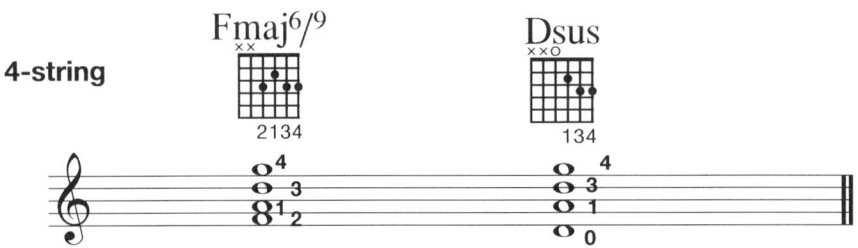

PRACTICE PROGRESSIONS #5

Use special-case chords.

1)

| Emin⁷ | Gmaj | Asus⁷ | Cmaj⁹ |

2)

| Dsus | Fmaj⁶/⁹ | Cmaj⁹ | Asus⁷ |

3)

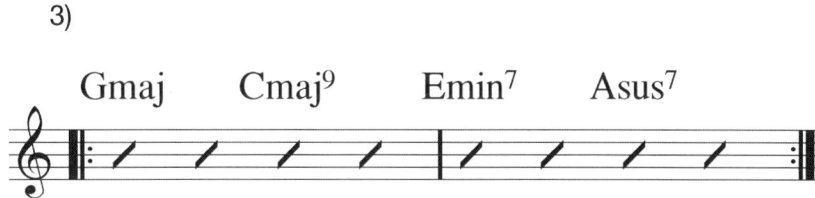

| Gmaj | Cmaj⁹ | Emin⁷ | Asus⁷ |

4)

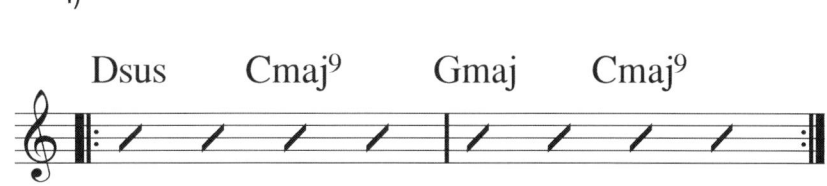

| Dsus | Cmaj⁹ | Gmaj | Cmaj⁹ |

Introduction To Barre Forms

There are two basic barre forms from which most of the moveable chords found in popular music are derived. They are the G major and C major forms.

These chords are the base chords from which all pop and rock electric guitar music is built.

The G Major and Minor forms are derived from the E maj & minor open position chord. There is one note difference between the two found in the 2nd finger.

Use the studies in this Volume to practice these shapes.

G Major & G Minor

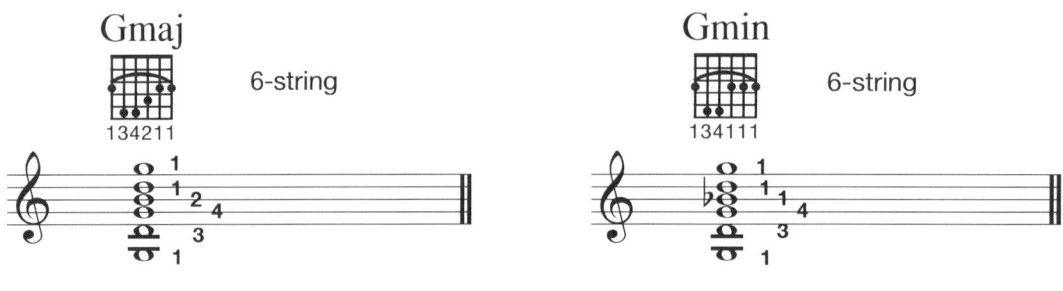

C Major & C Minor

The C major & minor forms are derived from the A major open position chord.

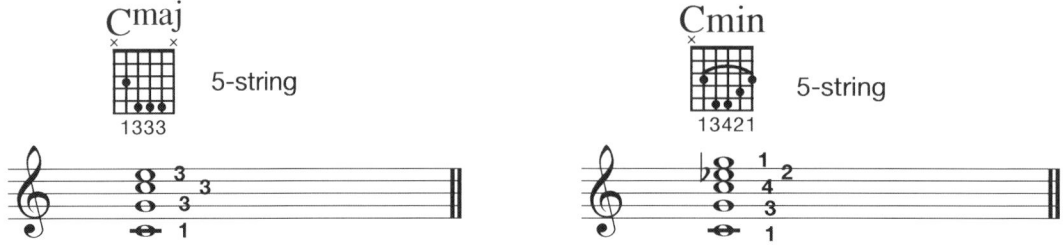

SUPPLEMENTAL CHAPTERS

CHAPTER 8

Rhythm Guitar Workouts

An ameture practices something until he gets it right.

A professional practices until he can't get it wrong!

- **Unknown** -

RHYTHM WORKOUT #1

Play only one chord throughout
Play one chord every 2 bars
Play one chord every bar

Mute the strings on the rests.

Example 1-one chrd every 2 bars

Example 2-one chrd every bar

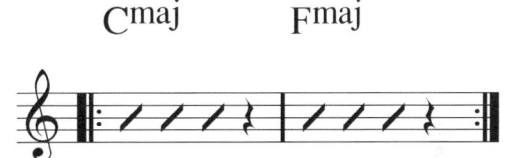

Quater Note Studies

1)

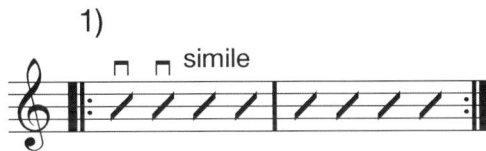

2)

3)

4)

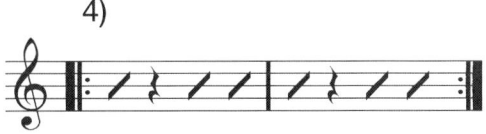

5)

6)

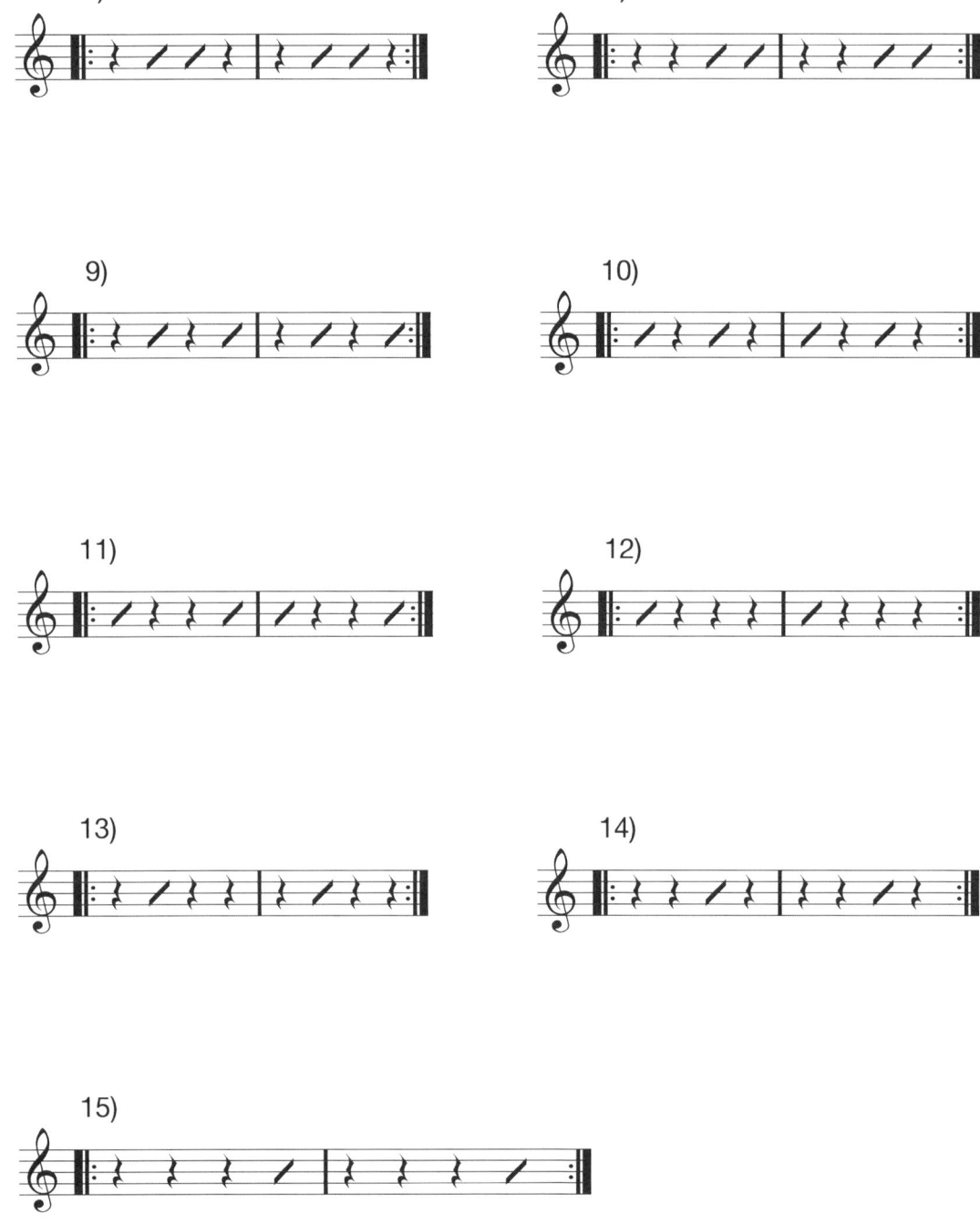

Tied Note Studies

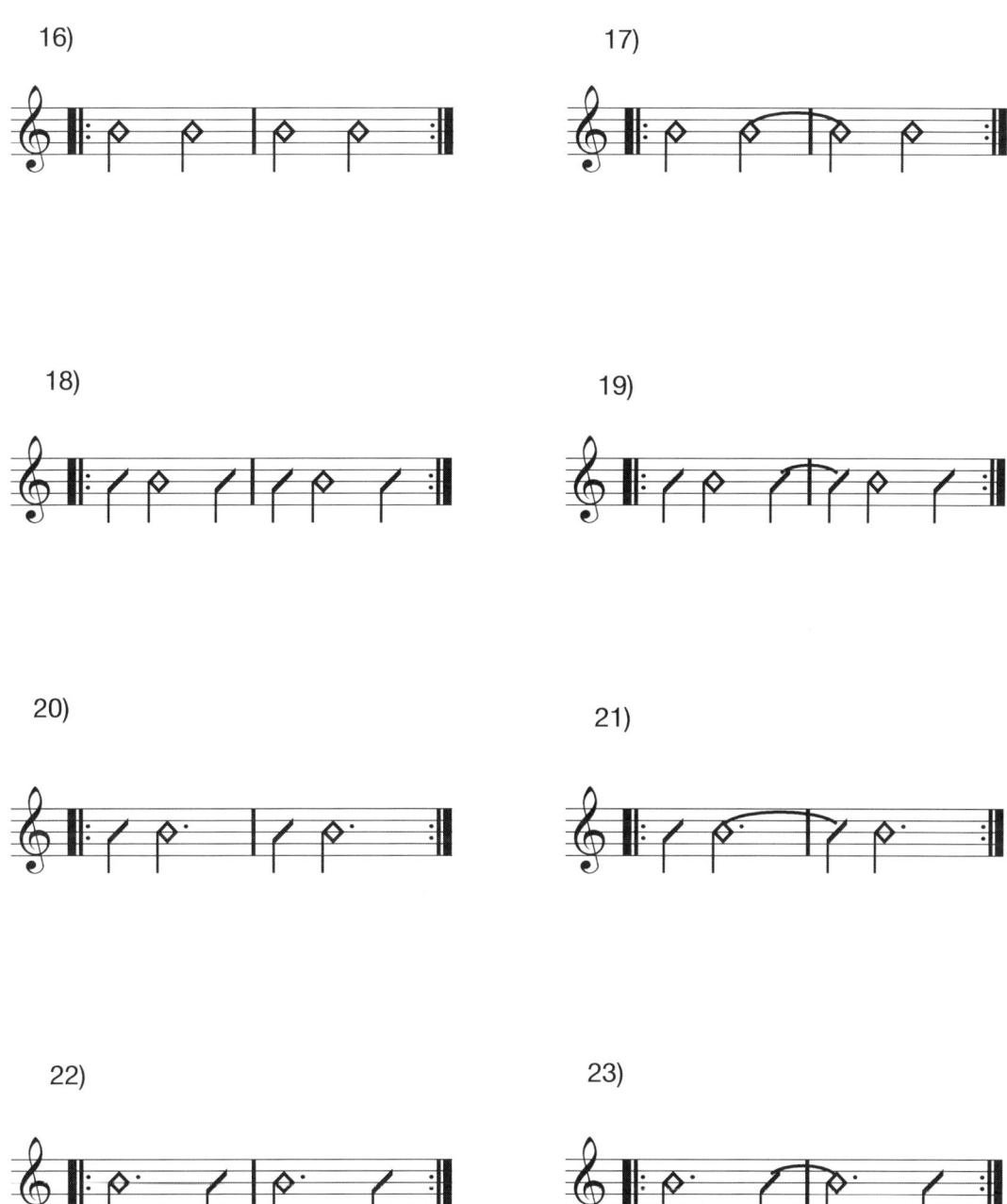

Eighth Note Studies

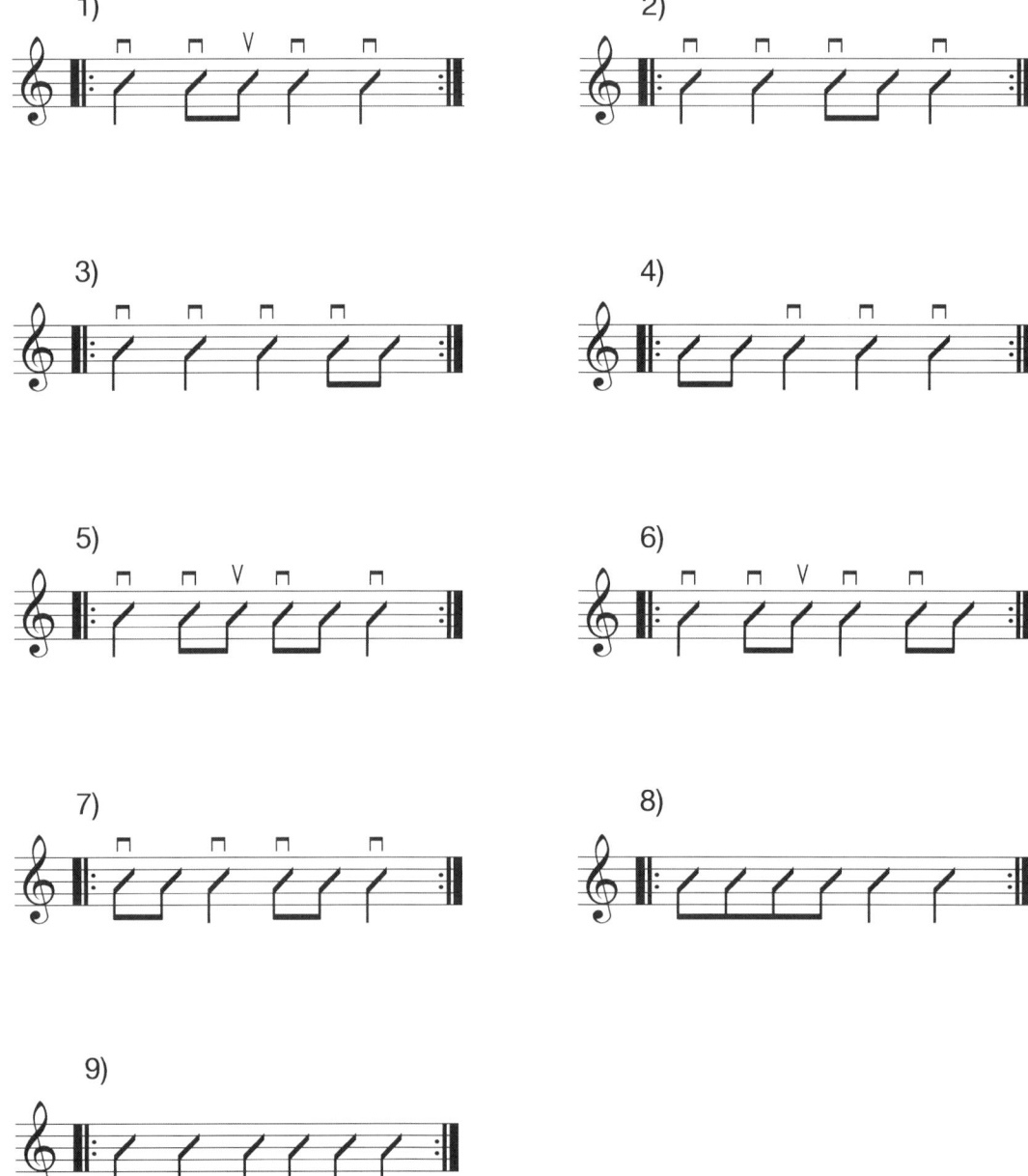

10)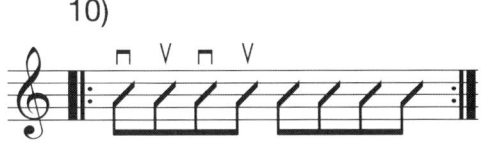

11)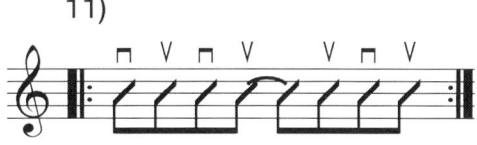

12)

13)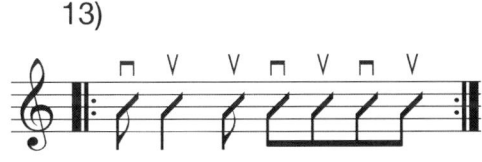

14)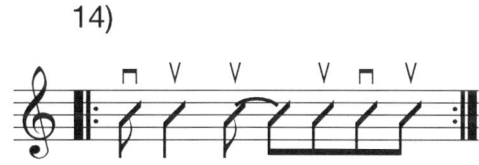

15)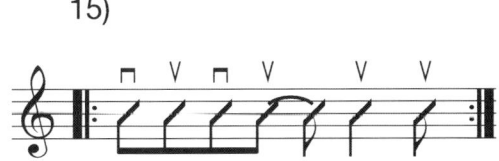

16)

PRACTICE PROGRESSIONS #6

1)

2)

3)

4)

5)

6)

7)

8)

9)

Bmaj, B7, Bmin Chords

The B major and B minor chords crop up occcasionally in different tunes. They are played mostly when performing tunes in the key of E. One way around this chord is to use a capo which transposes it so the open-string chors become available. The preferred way is to learn these forms listed below.

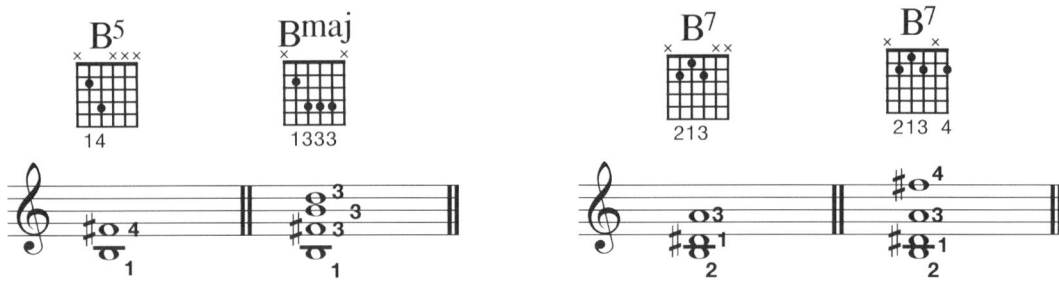

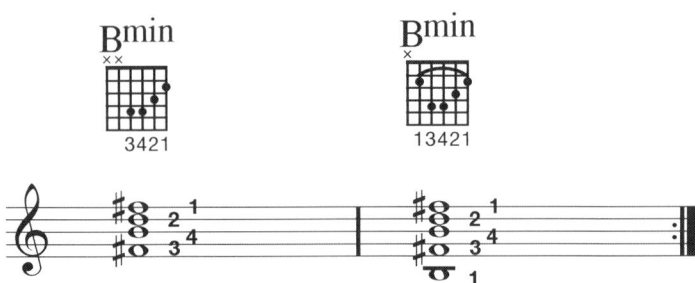

*Since God made us
to be originals,
why stoop
to be a copy.*

-Rev. Billy Graham-

CHAPTER 9

Introduction To Fingerpicking

*An Artist can not fail.
It is a success just to be one.*

- Charles Horton Cooley -

*Hangin' in there?
Keep goin', it's worth it!*

Right Hand Positioning

This is an overview of right hand finger groupings for all possible sets of strings using the thumb, index finger, middle finger and third finger. The customary finger designations for guitar are p-i-m-a:

(p) - pollex or thumb
(i) - index
(m) - medius or middle
(a) - annularus or third

The right hand closes very naturally with a slight rotation of the wrist as the fingers collapse in laterally. The thumb moves upward. This motion is similar to the turning of a thumb screw. Keep the right hand close to the strings.

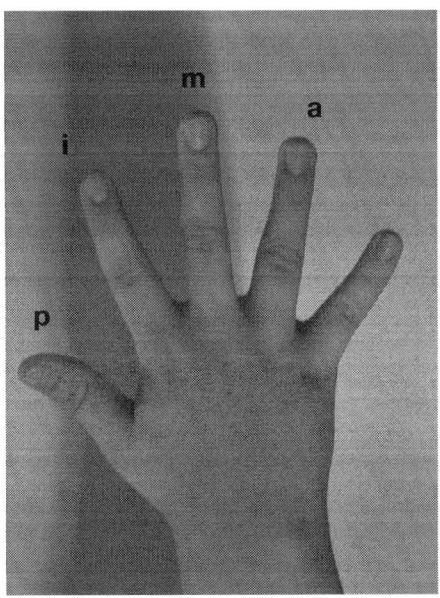

Placing The Right Hand

1. Place the right forearm so it lays slightly above the front face of the guitar with the elbow joint on the top front edge of the guitar. The forearm will be at an approximate 45 degree angle to the floor. The right hand thumb is located center to the sound hole.

2. The wrist is at a slight sideways rotation towards the guitar which angles the left finger tips of (i) and (m) across the string while (a) remains perpendicular to the string. Keep the wrist relatively flat towards the face of the guitar.

3. The left tip of the thumb remains slightly forward from the index finger and is relaxed, hanging in a natural position not touching the strings.

4. Both shoulders are relaxed with the right shoulder slightly lowered form the left shoulder. Avoid dropping the right shoulder too low which will cause the right elbow to move from its location at the top front edge of the guitar. This will cause the right hand to move too far back from the sound hole. Stay relaxed and natural.

RH Finger Groups

129

There are three variations to the Group 1 fingering set. The first three (i,m,a) fingers remain stationary on strings 1-2-3 as the thumb moves to each bass string (4, 5, 6) respectively.

This action prompts correct placement of fingers on the strings which is a set up for the next finger activation exercises. The technique is similar to the chordal and arpeggio playing found in piano. All strings are either sounded at one time in one strike or they are activated individually by each finger.

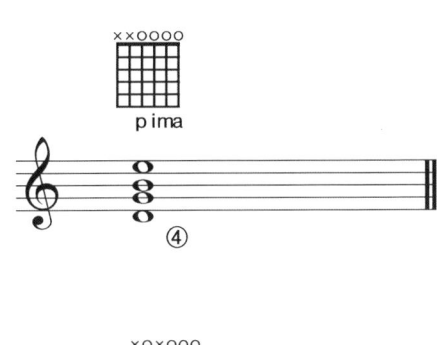

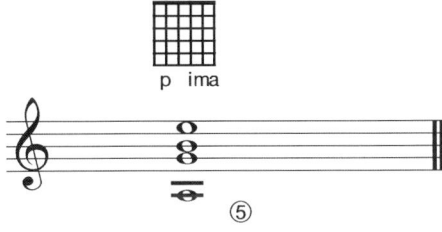

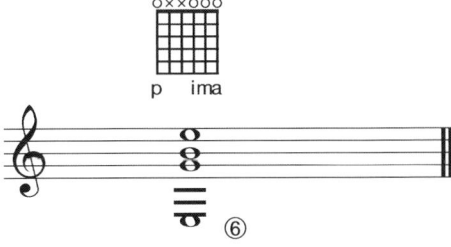

Group 1 RH Fingers

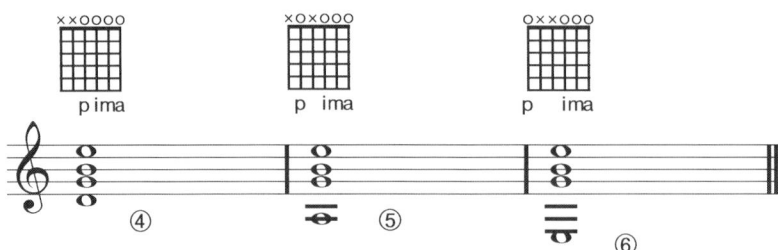

Study 9.1
Groupings

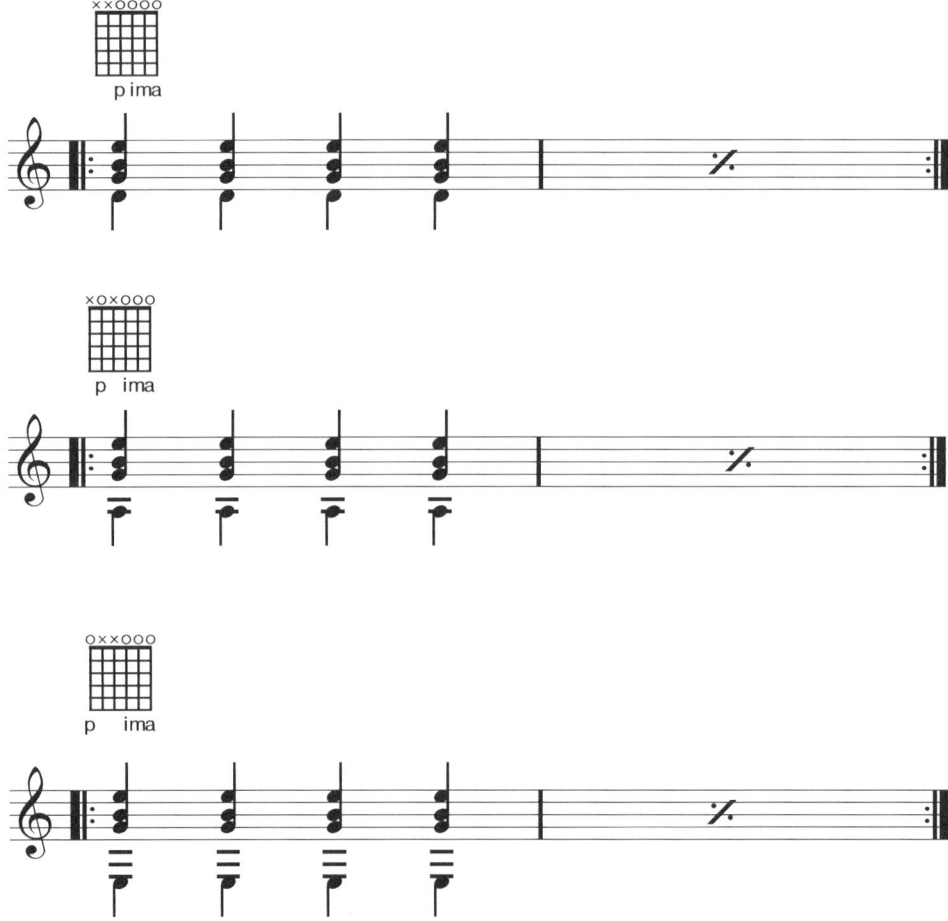

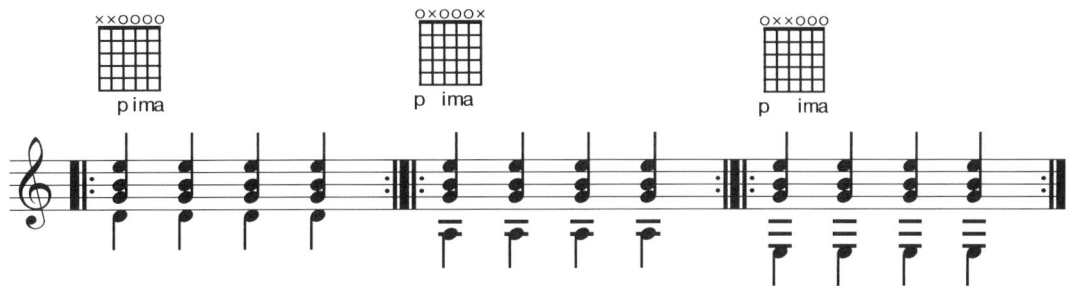

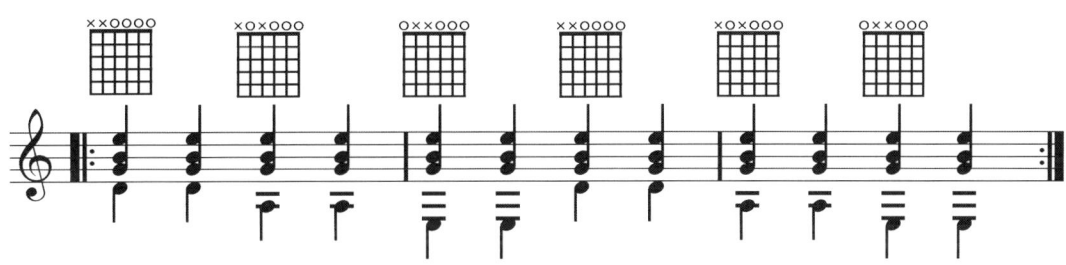

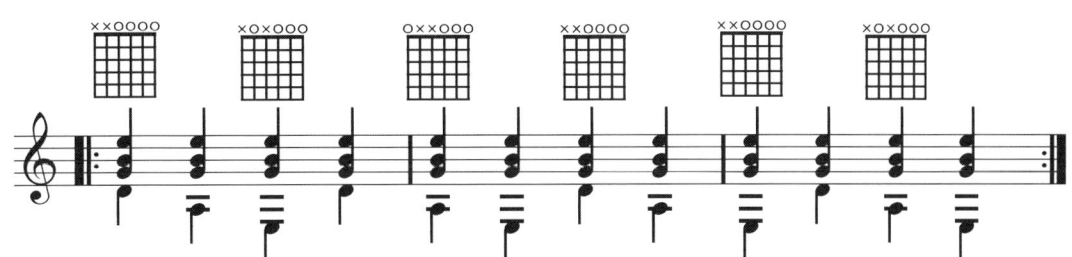

Study 9.2
Forward Activation

The following examples use a forward finger activation using the previous finger groupings.

Study 9.2a
Applied

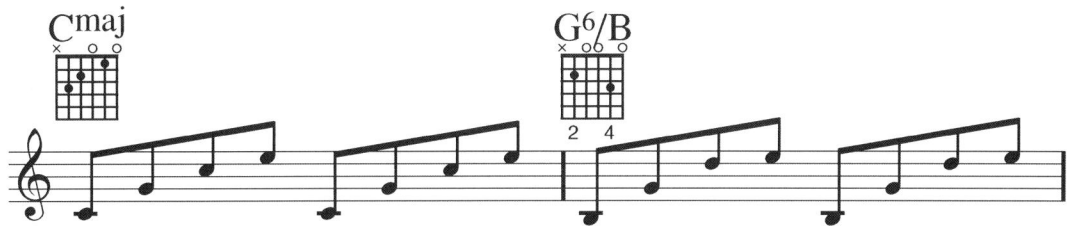

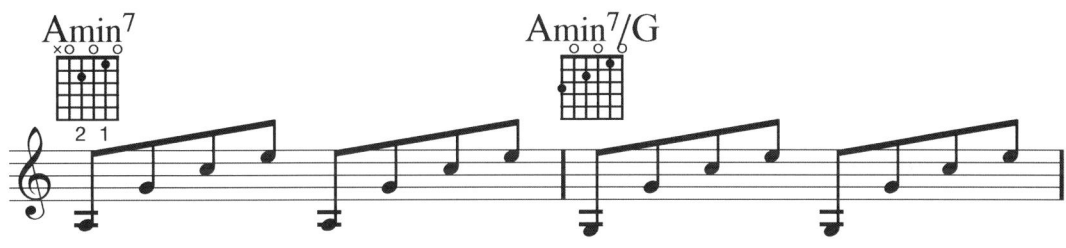

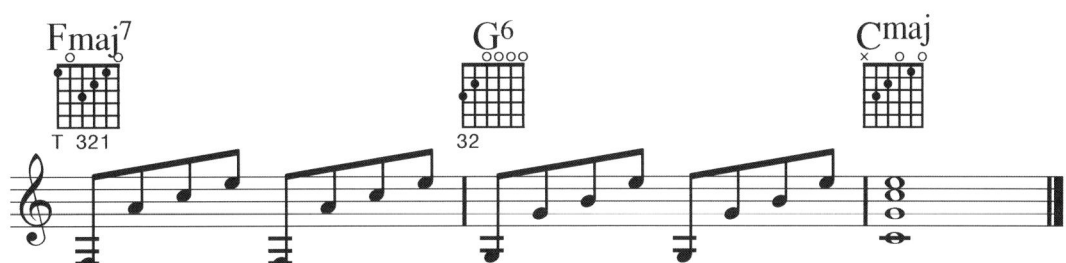

Study 9.3
Arc Activation

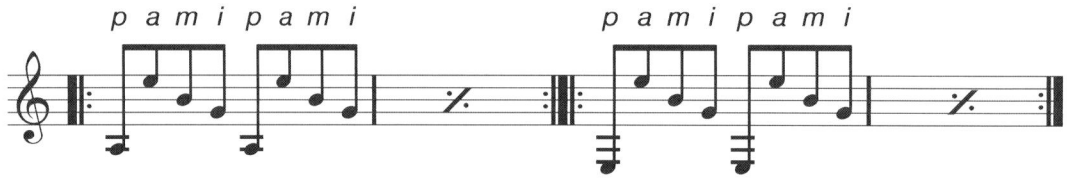

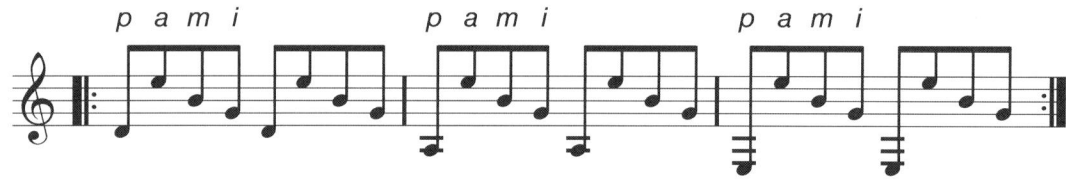

Study 9.3a
Applied

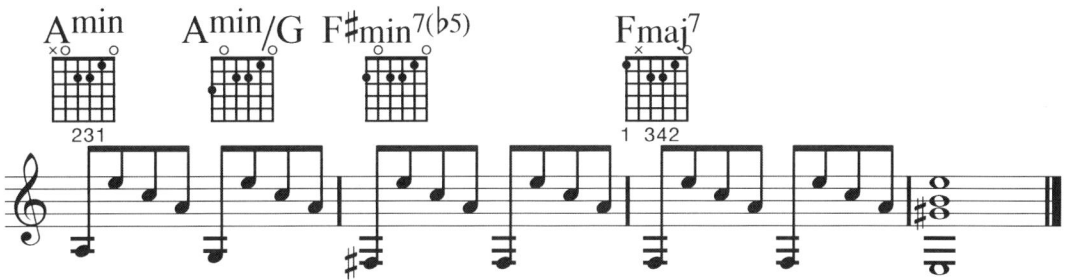

Study 9.4
Carcassi Activation

Study 9.4a
Applied

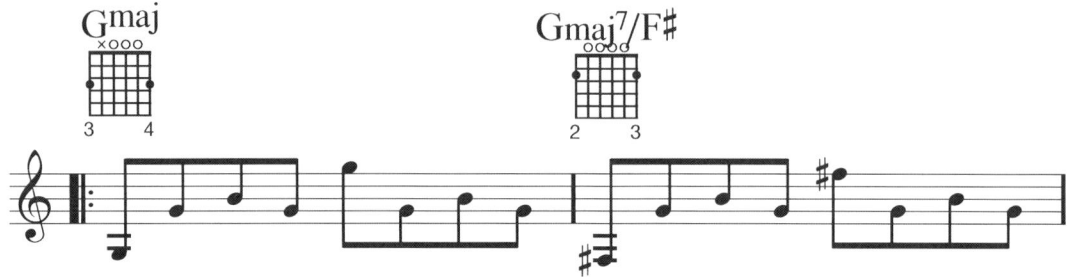

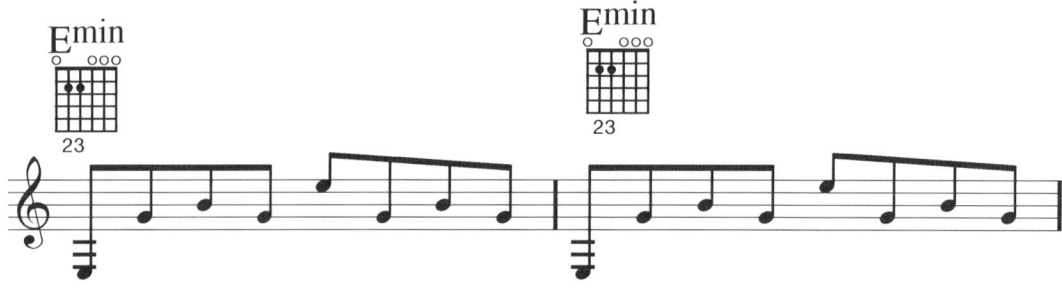

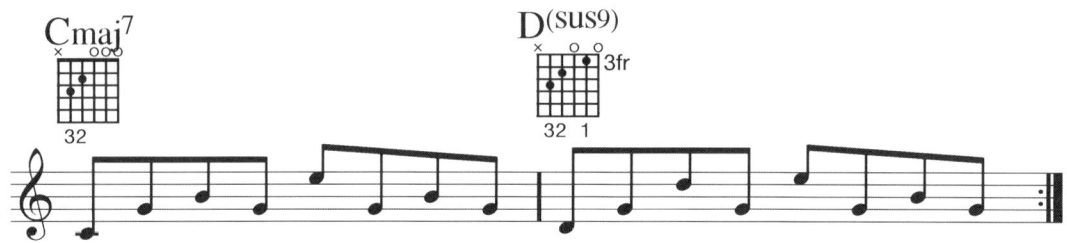

CHAPTER 10

Practice Tunes

Some one told Chet Atkins, " Man that guitar sounds good!"

Chet set the guitar down on a chair and asked him, "Okay, how does it sound now."

- Chet Atkins -

S.H.A.

KEY OF G:

KEY OF C:

KEY OF D:

KEY OF A:

T. J.

KEY OF G:

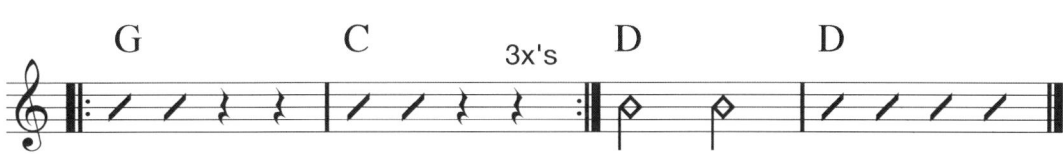

KEY OF C:

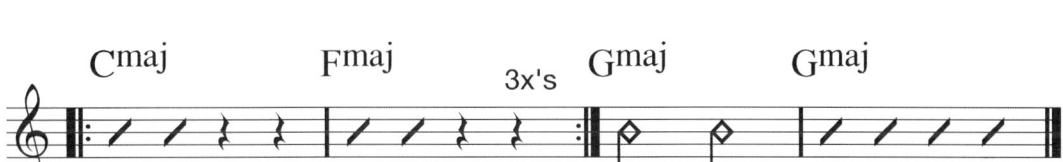

KEY OF D:

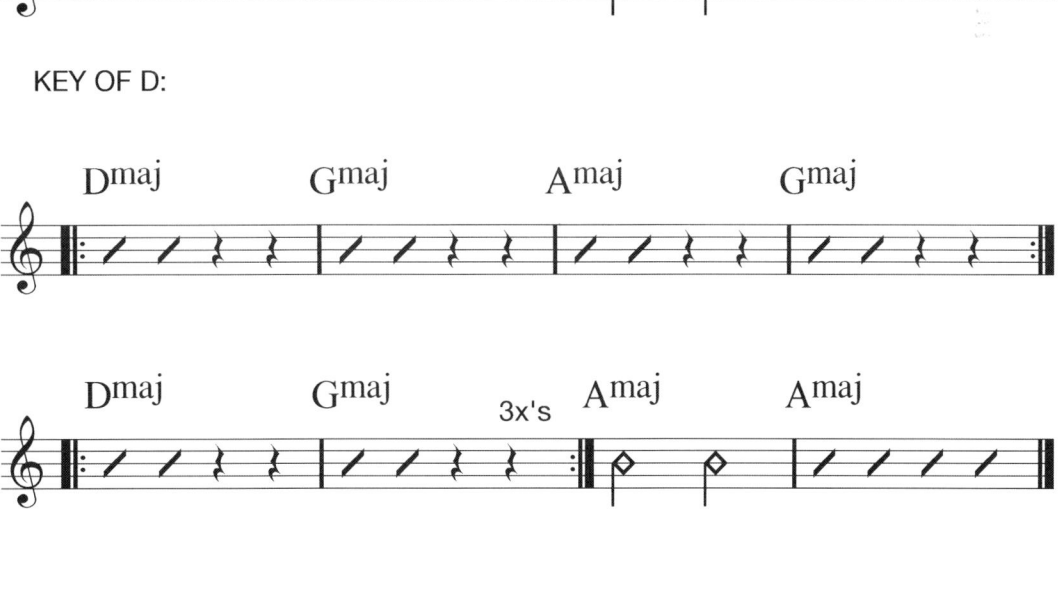

140
T. J.

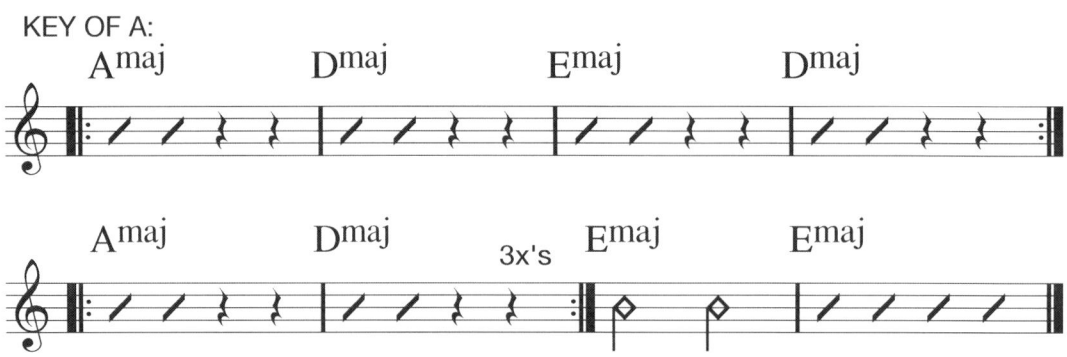

L. L.

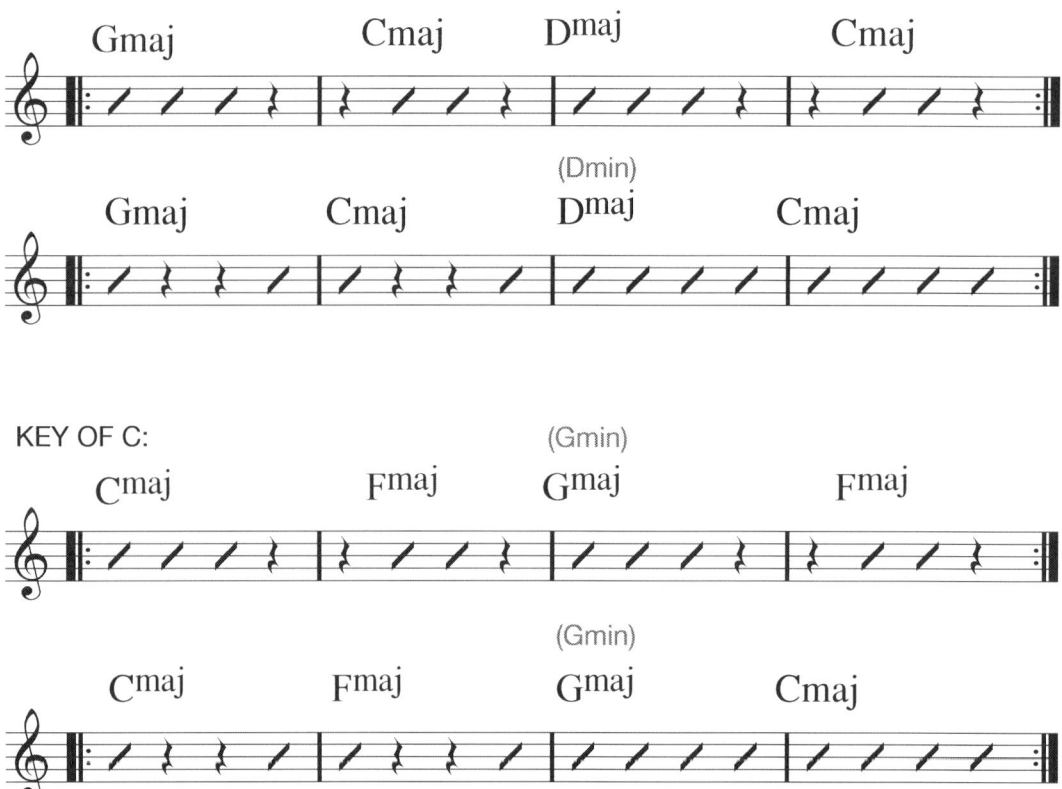

L. L.

KEY OF D:

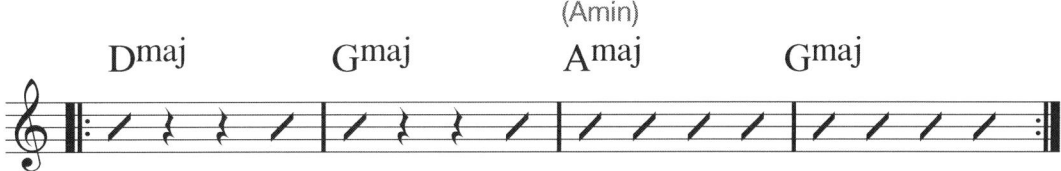

KEY OF A:

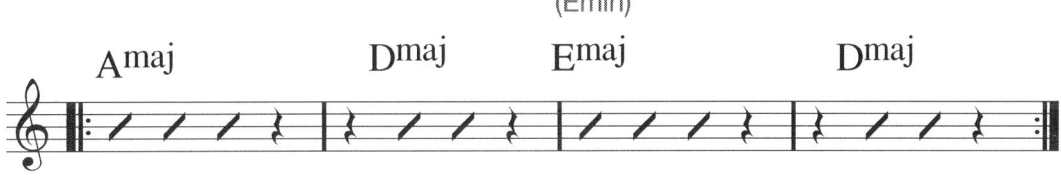

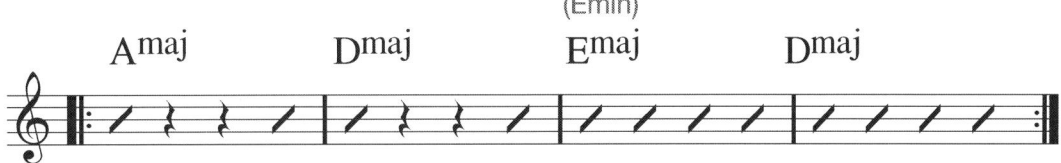

F. F.

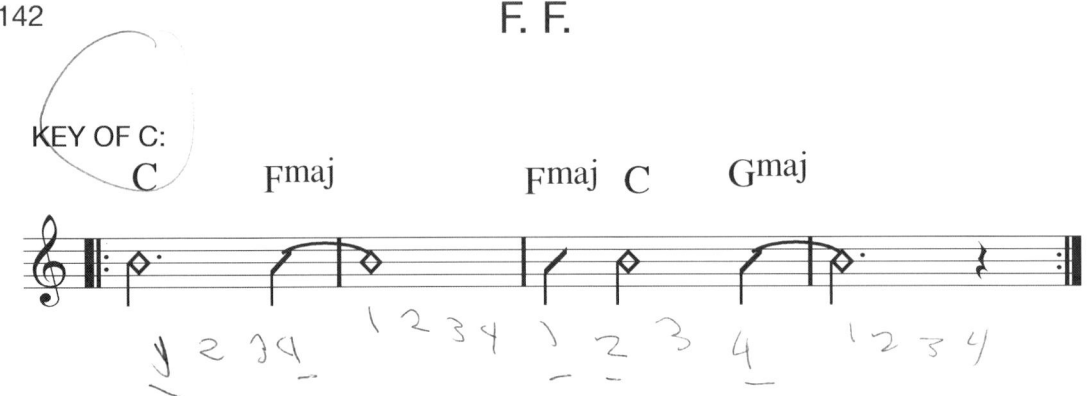

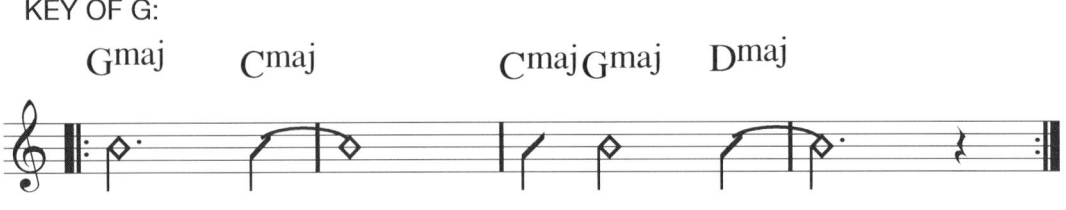

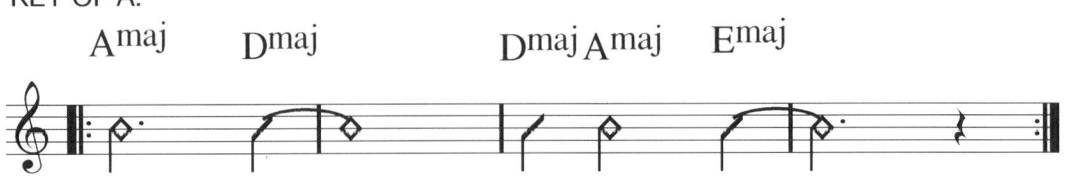

H. U. E. S. T. R.

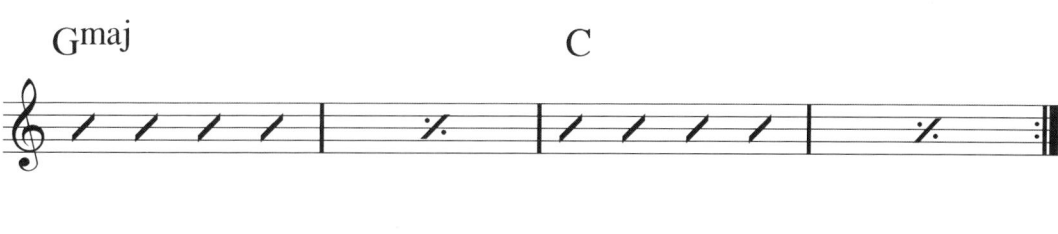

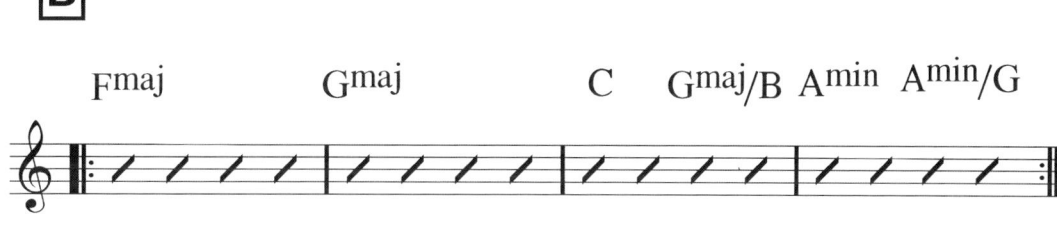

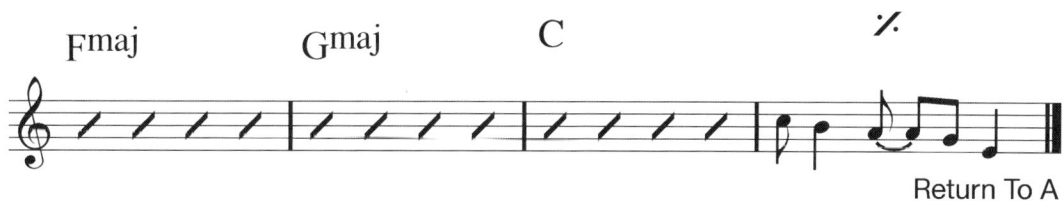

Return To A

WYGA

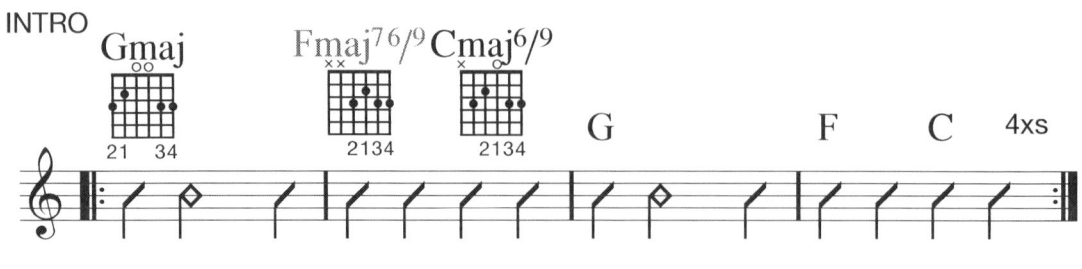

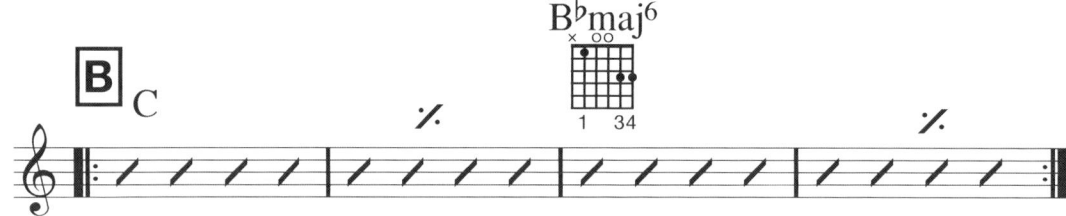

Return To A

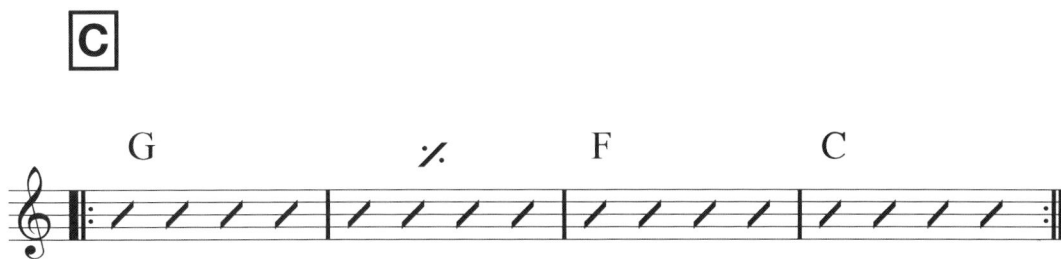

Return to Intro

H. J.

L.I. B.

A
C G Fmaj C
Cmaj Gmaj Fmaj Cmaj
B
Amin G Fmaj C
C G Fmaj C
D.C.

T & Shout

C F G
1 2 3 + 4 +
C F G

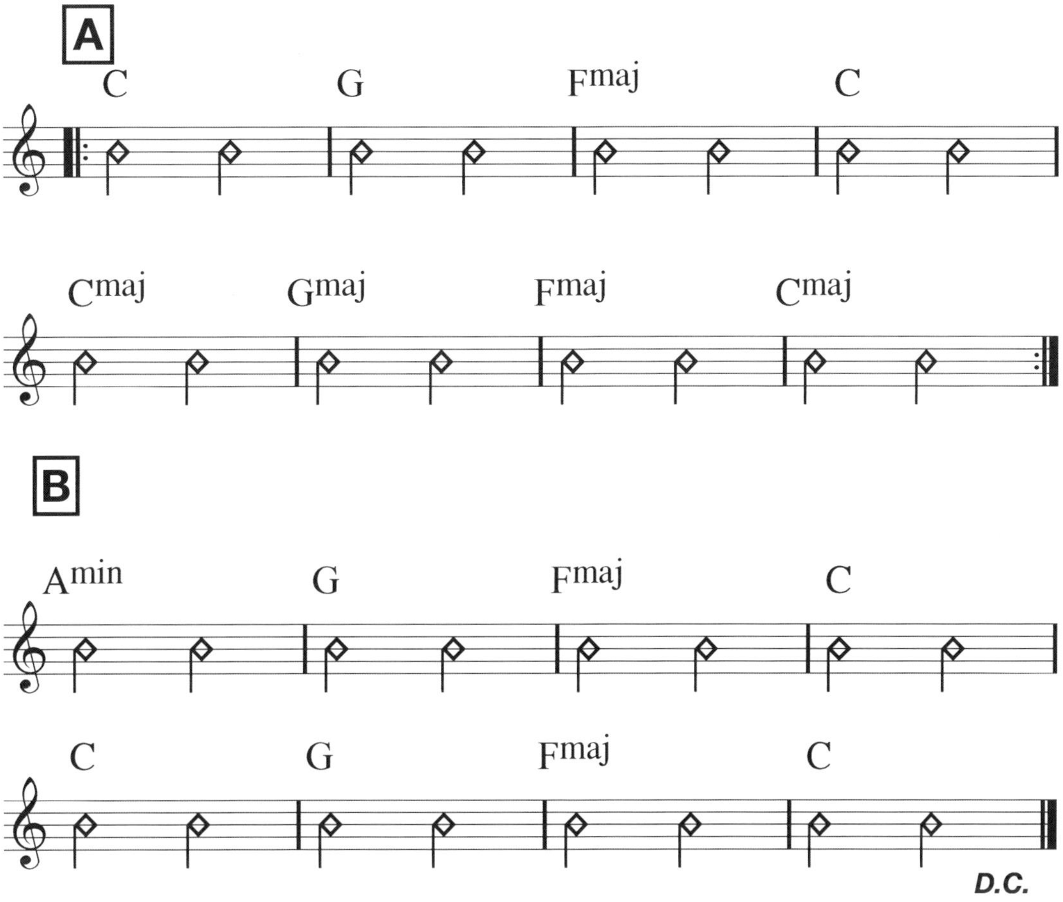

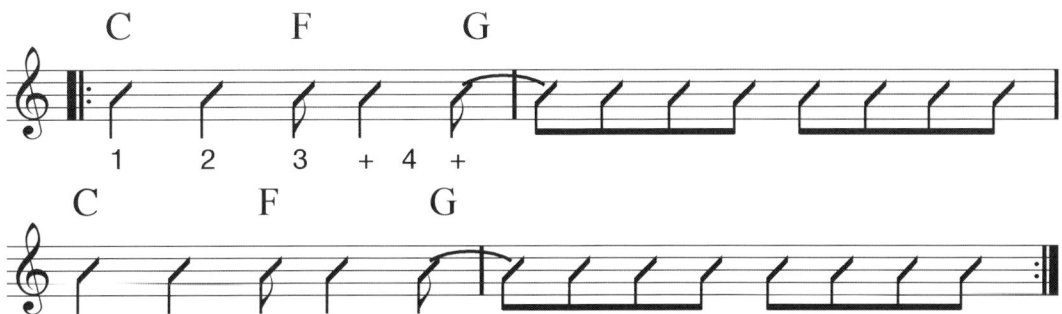

T. T. R.

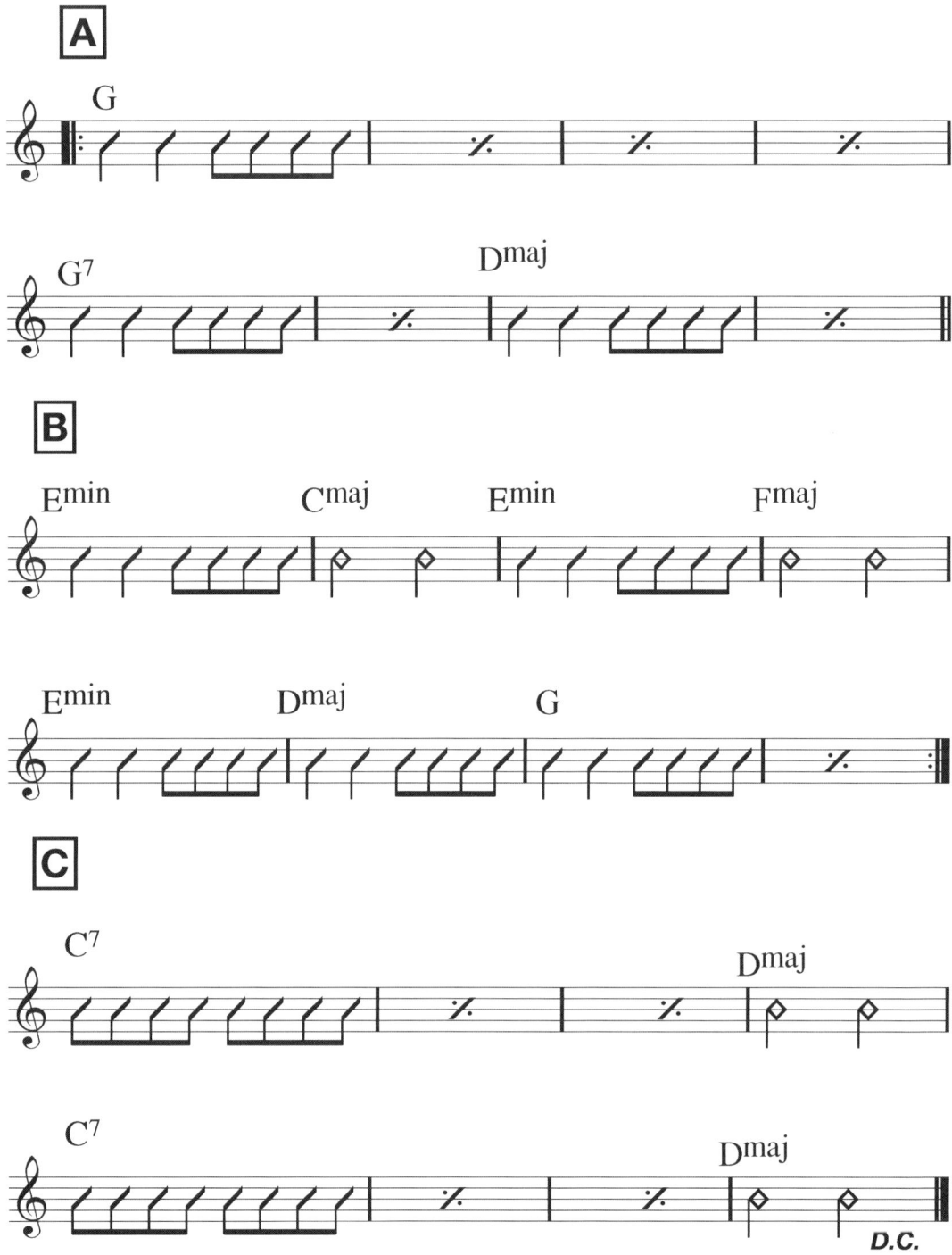

D. T.

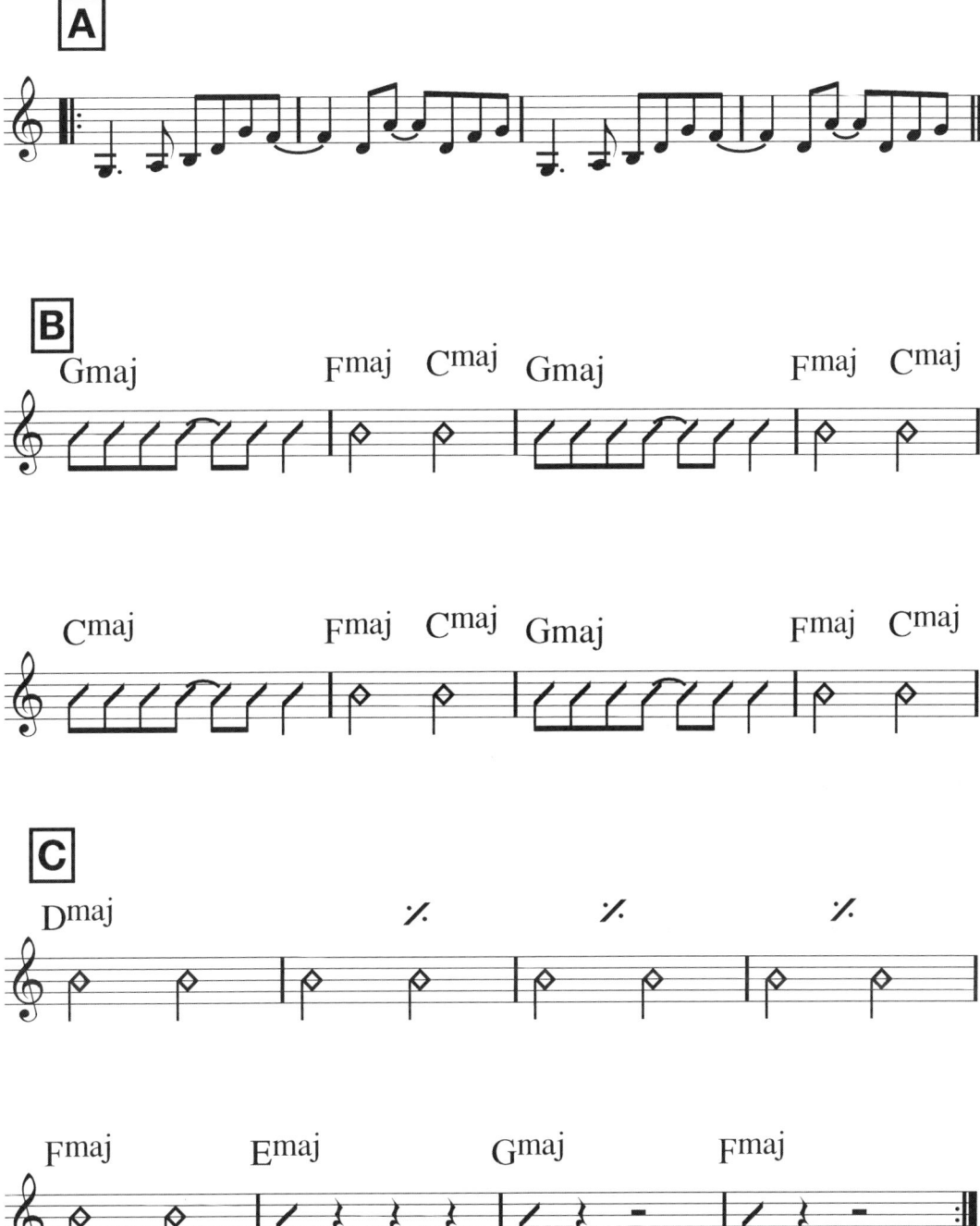

8 D.A.W.

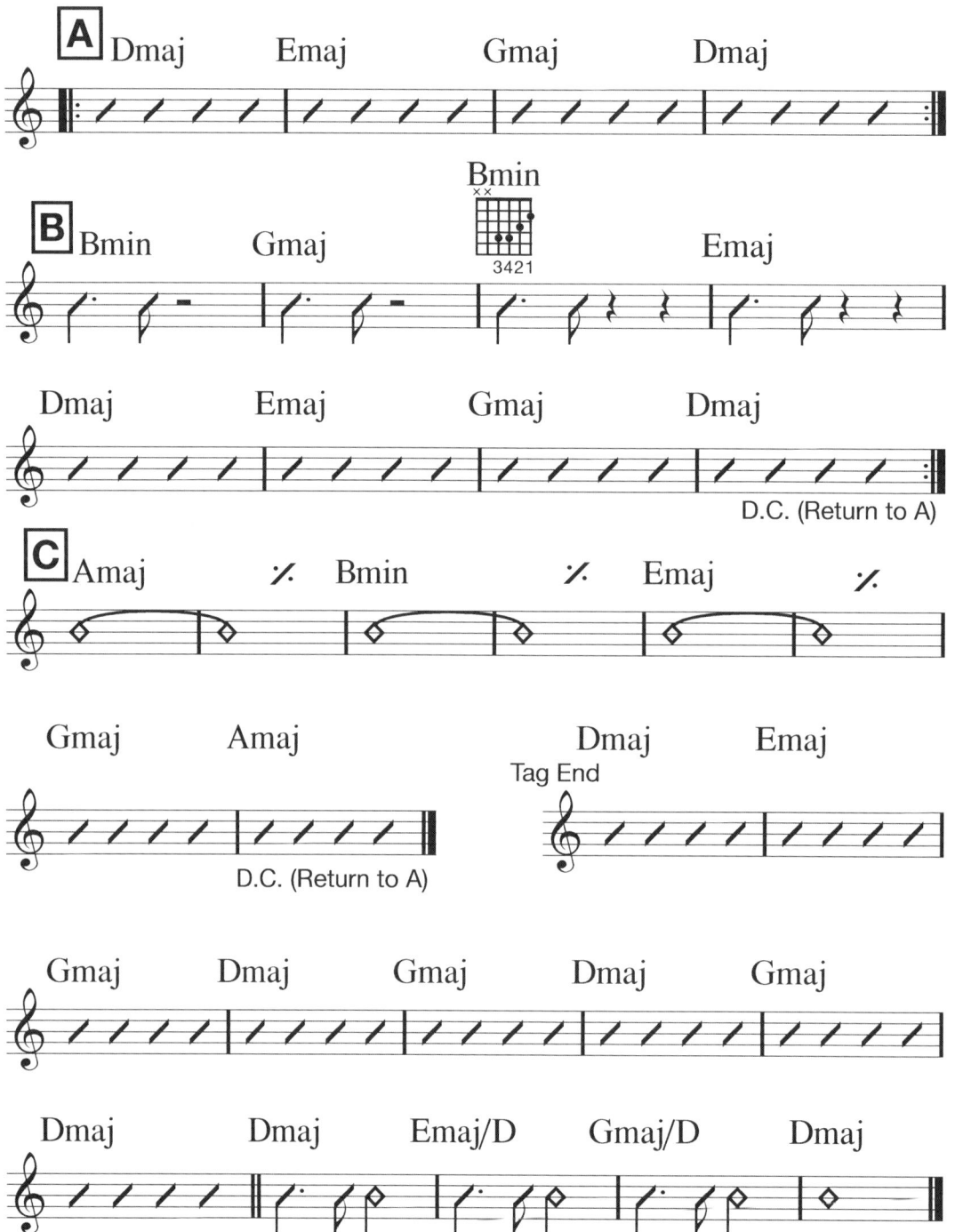

A.H.D.N.

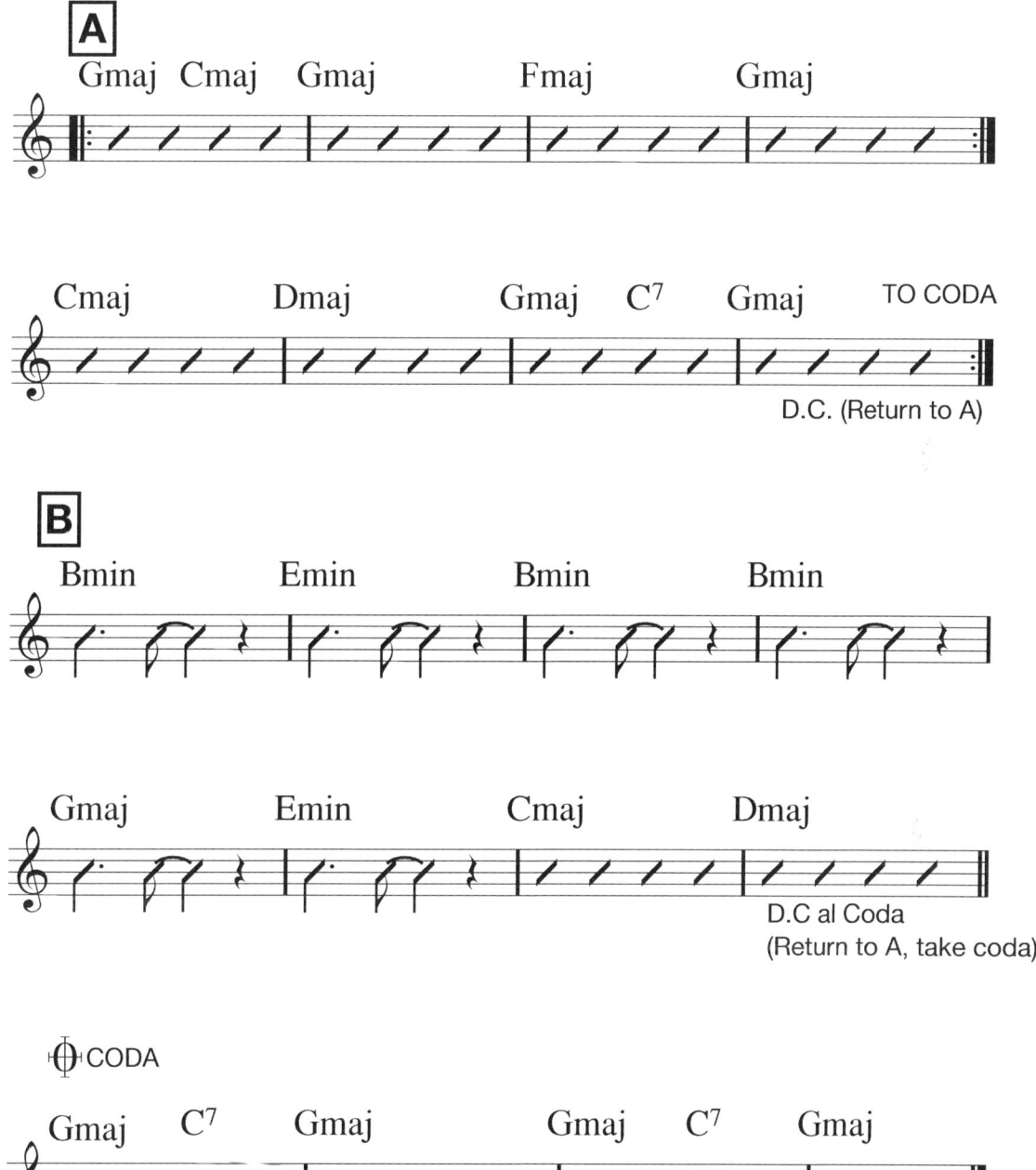

H. M.

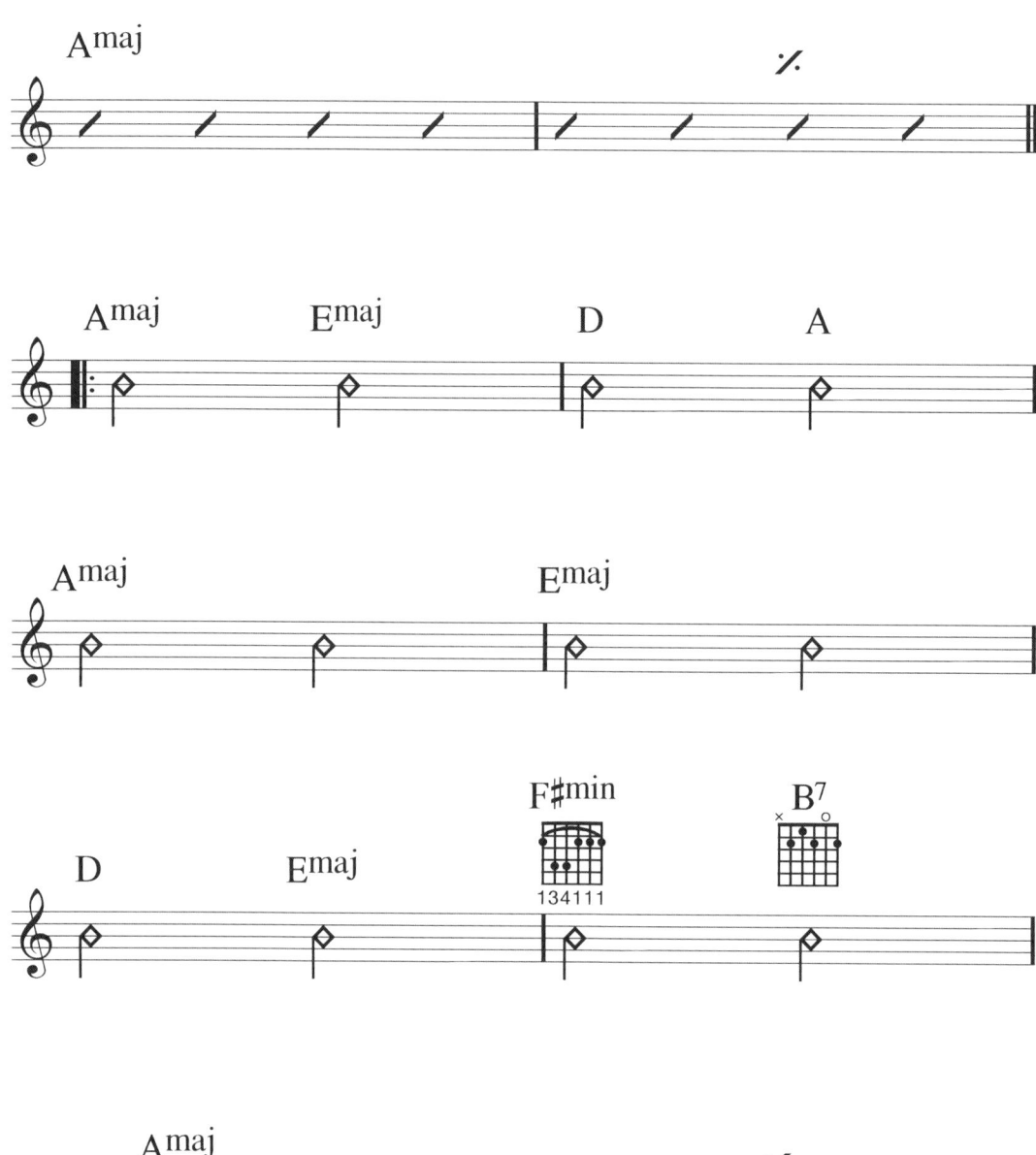

H.

4 D I O

O.M.

INTRO

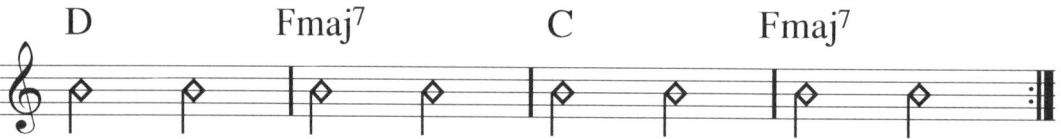

N & T D. D.

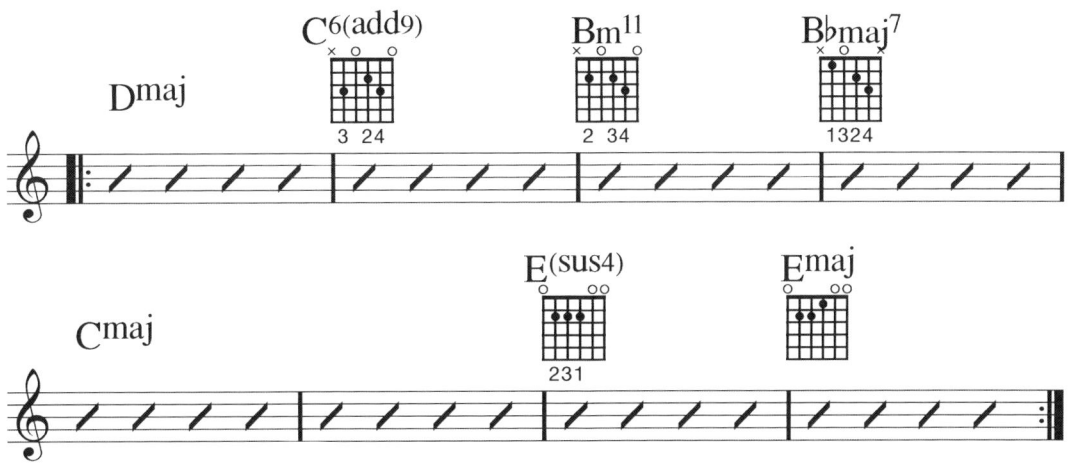

H. O. G.

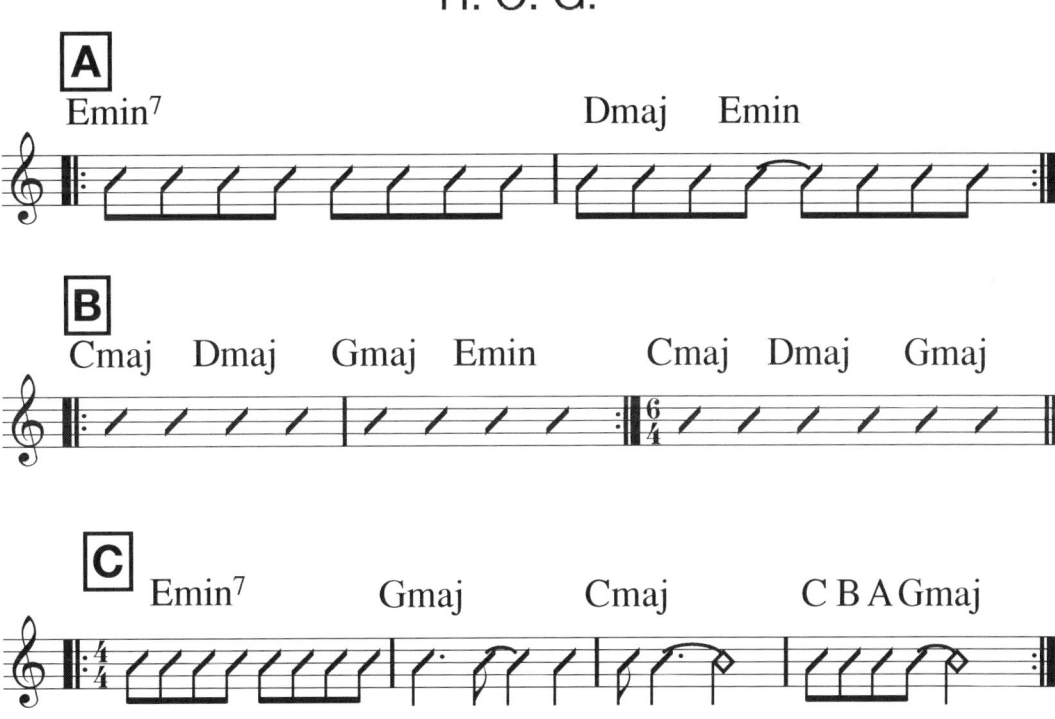

D.B.T. R.

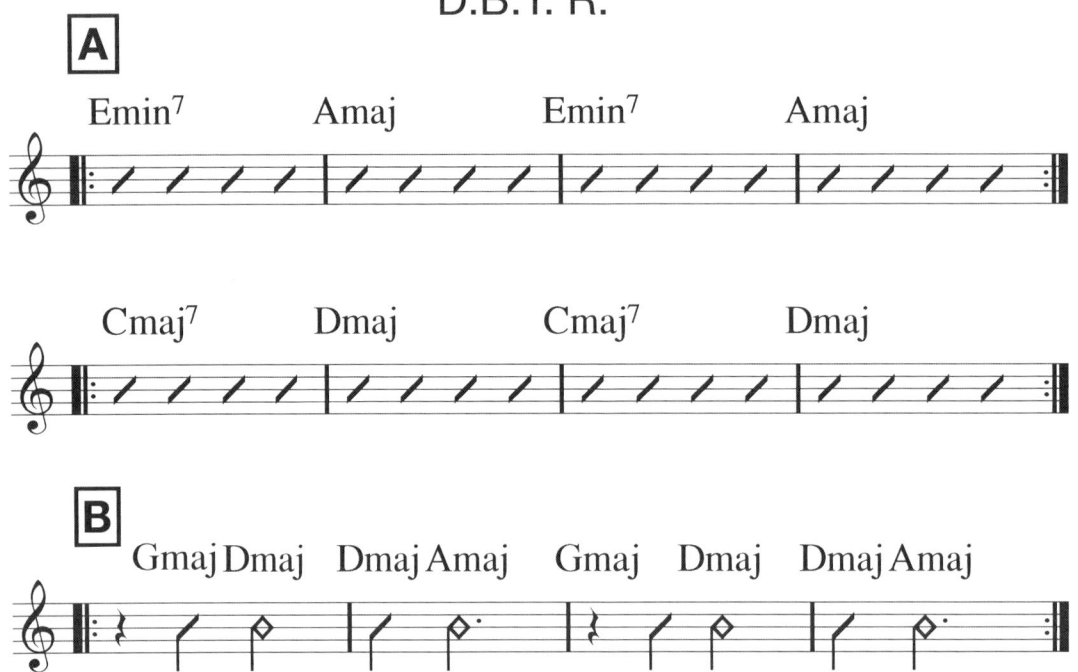

Standard Blues In A

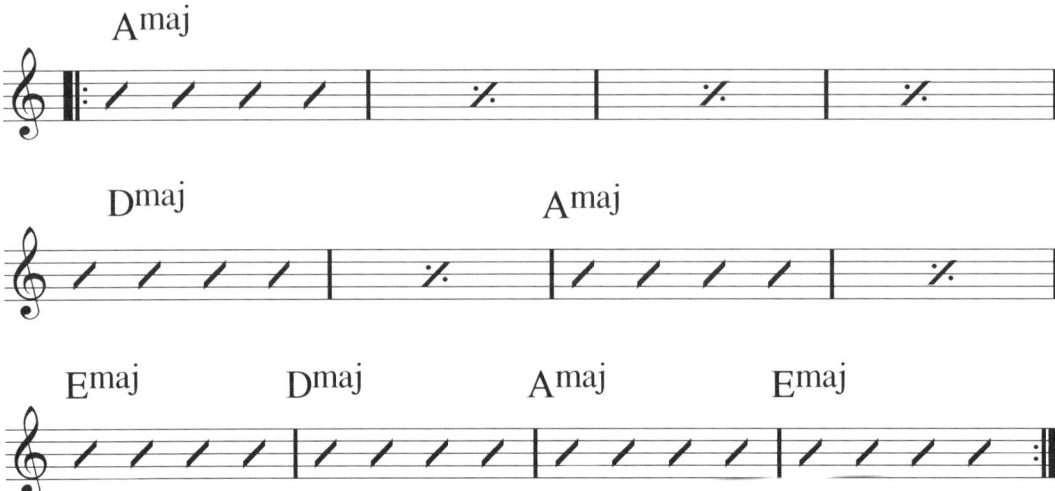

Standard Blues In E

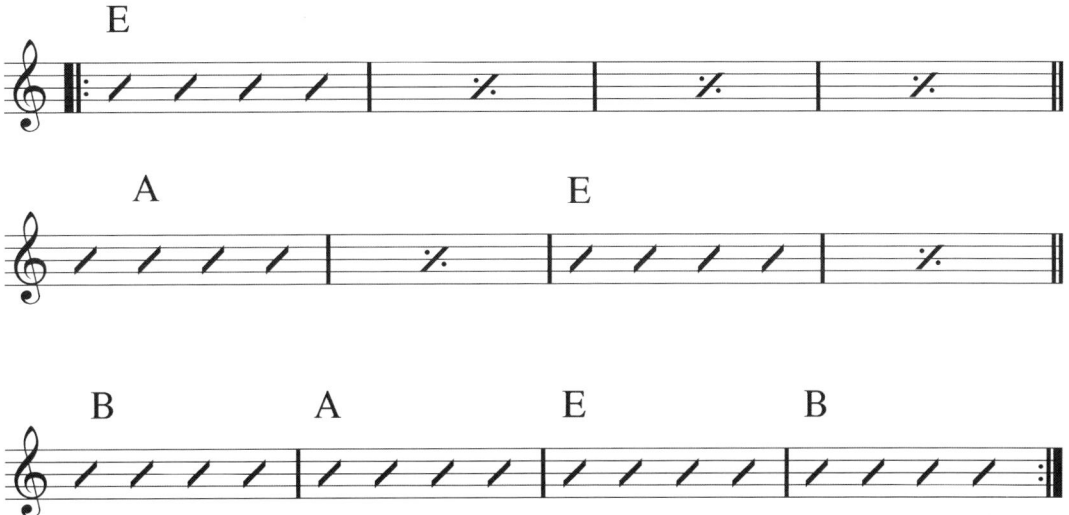

Standard Blues In G

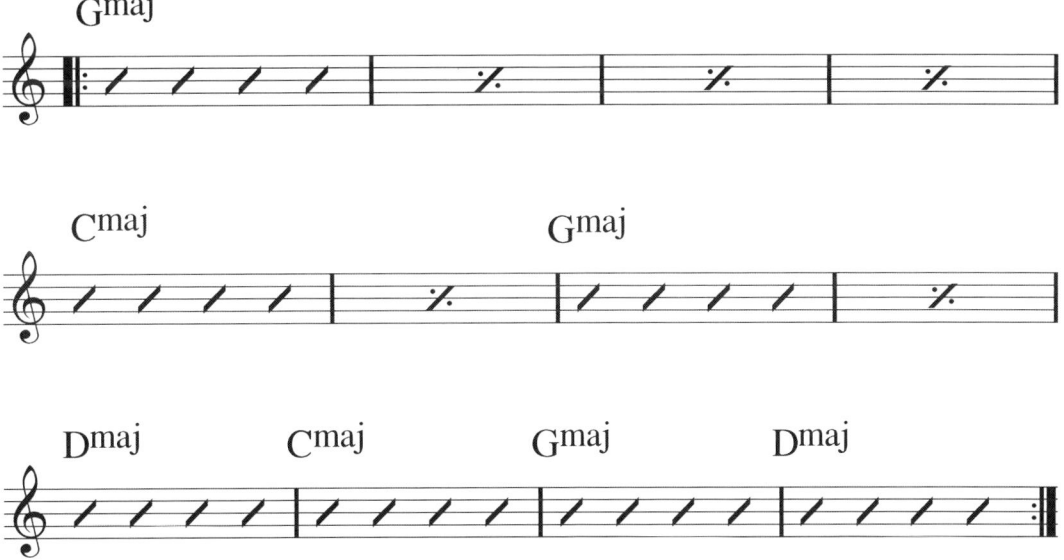

SBM

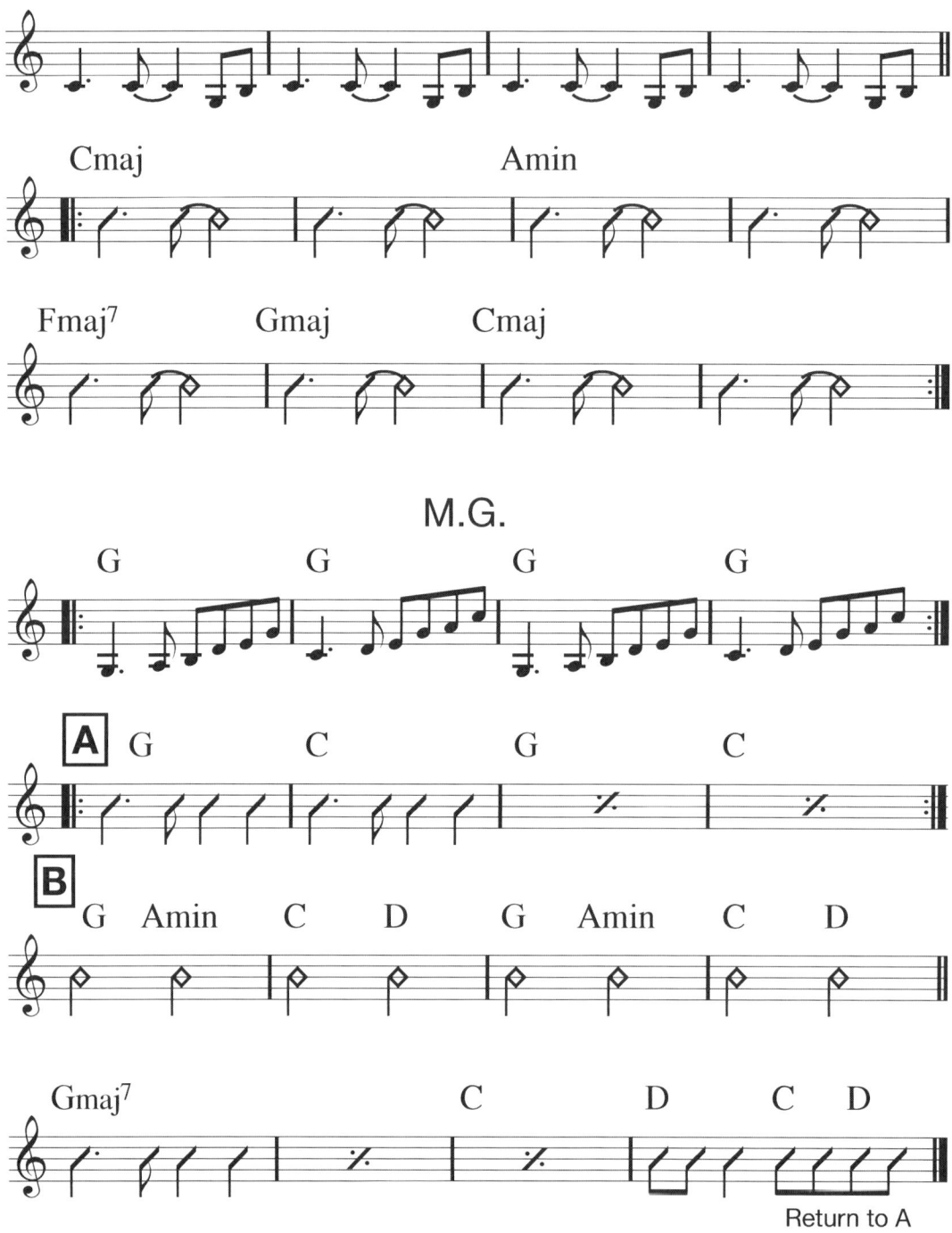

D.O.T.B.

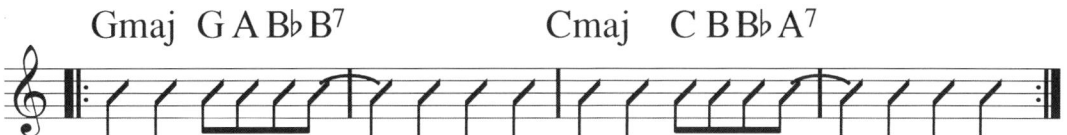

return to A and repeat

C. R.

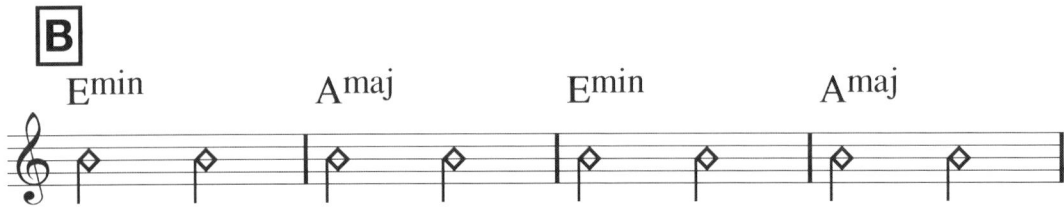

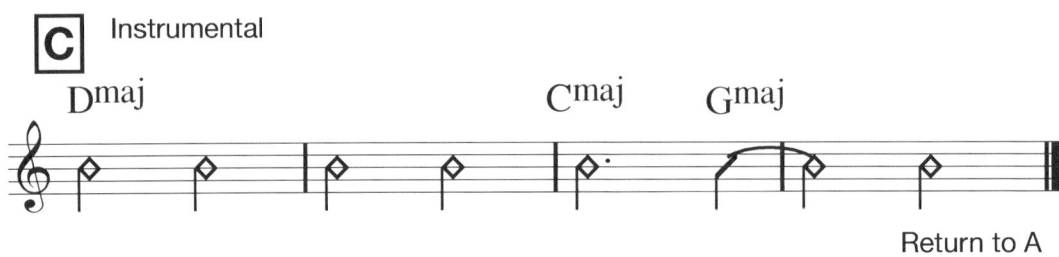

Return to A

Y.G.A.F.

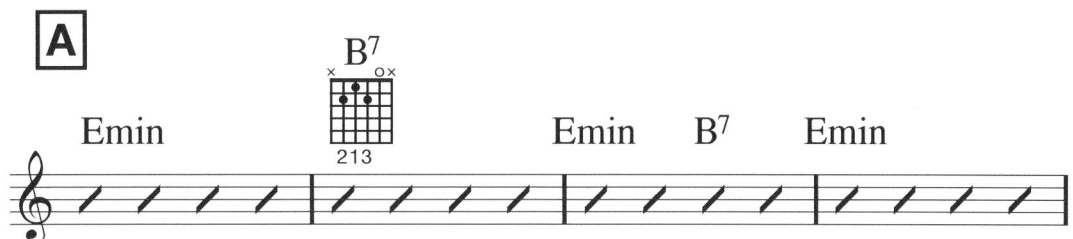

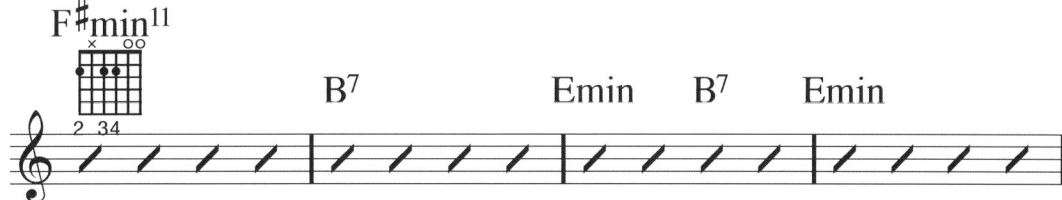

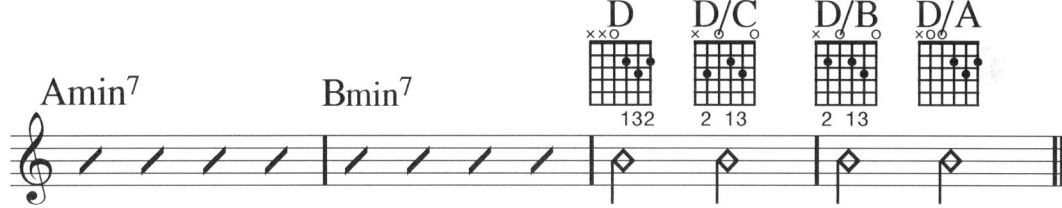

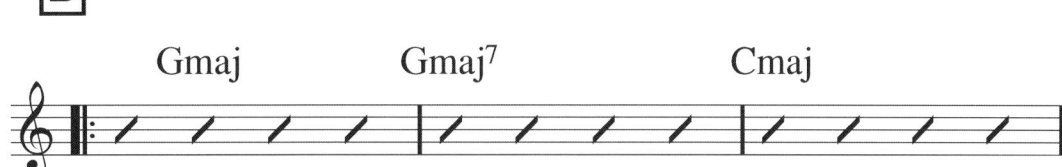

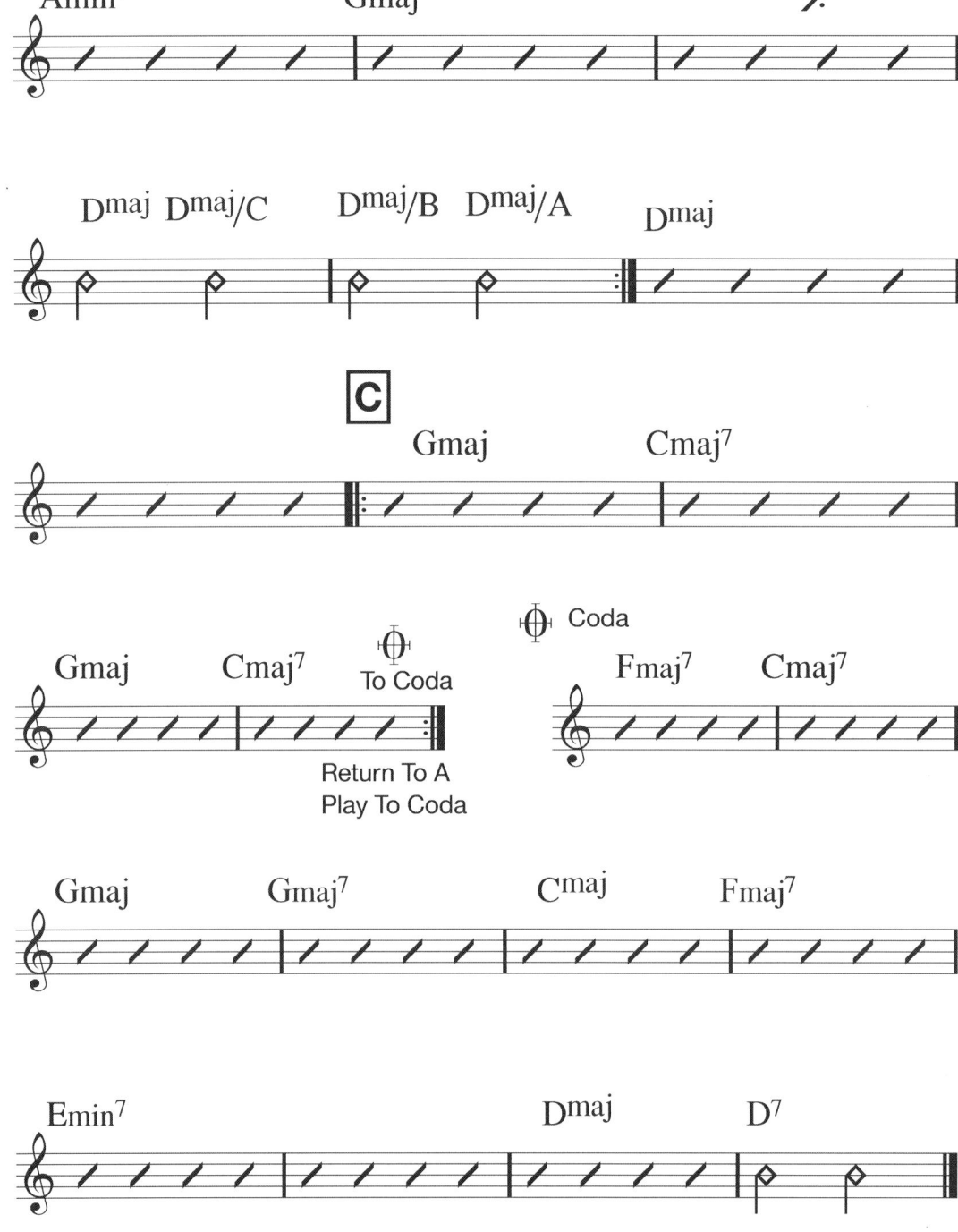

M.S.

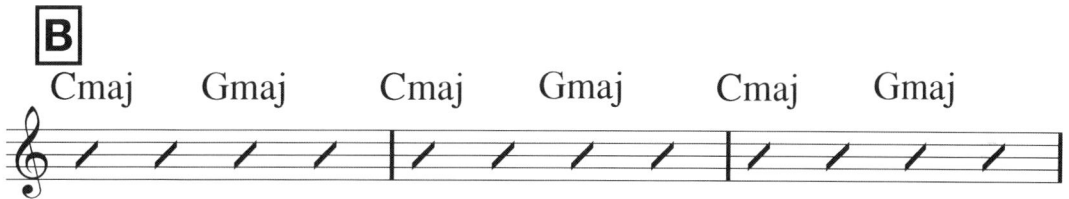

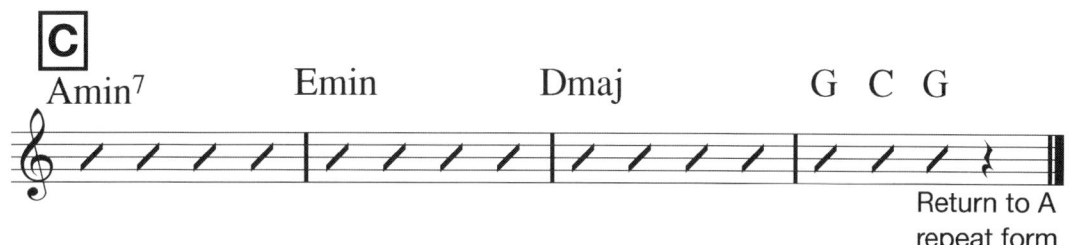

Return to A repeat form

L.O.A.J.P.

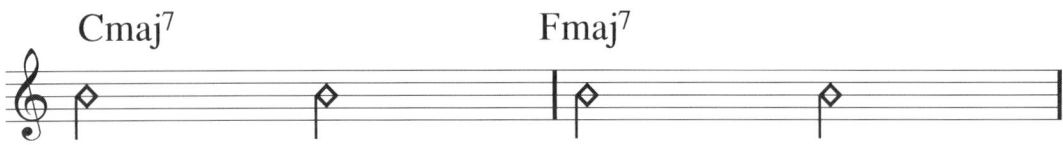

C. J.

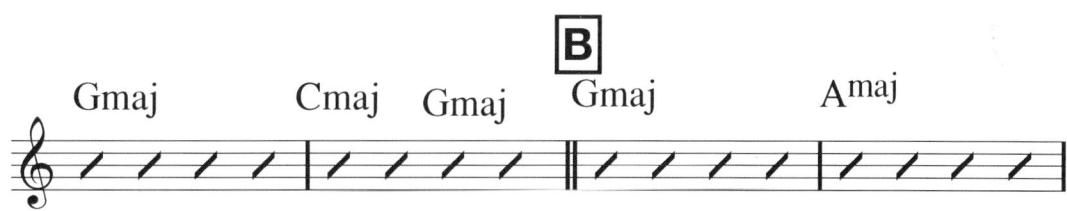

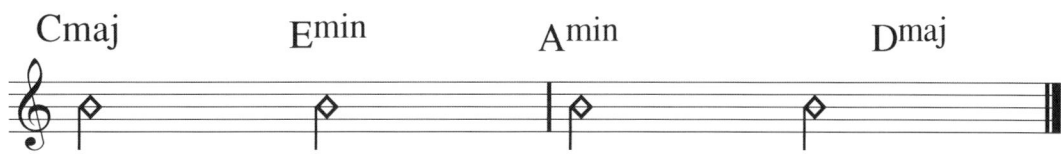

M & M U.

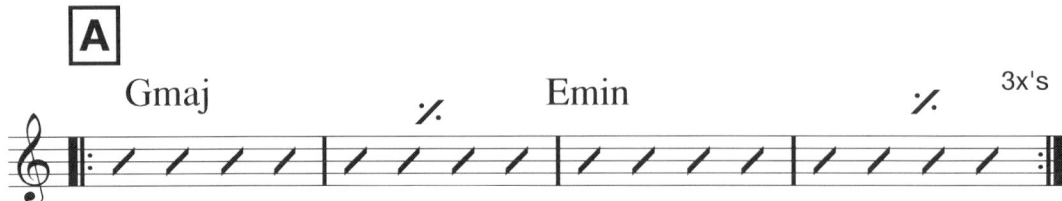

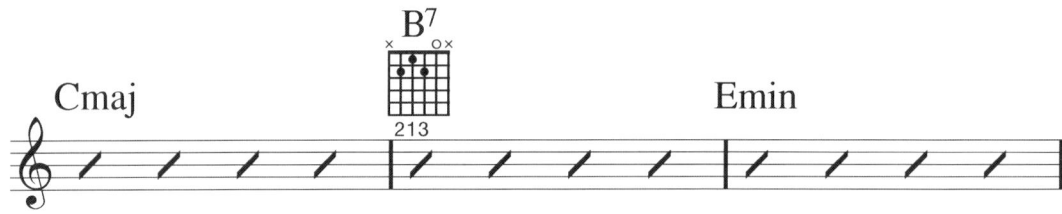
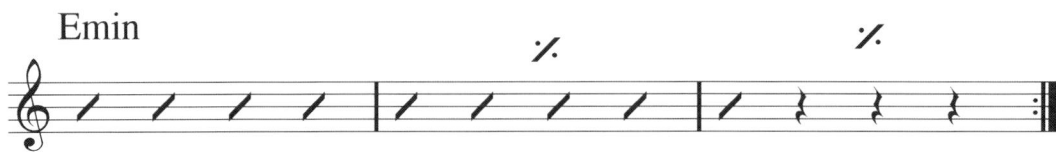

I.D.N.N.D.

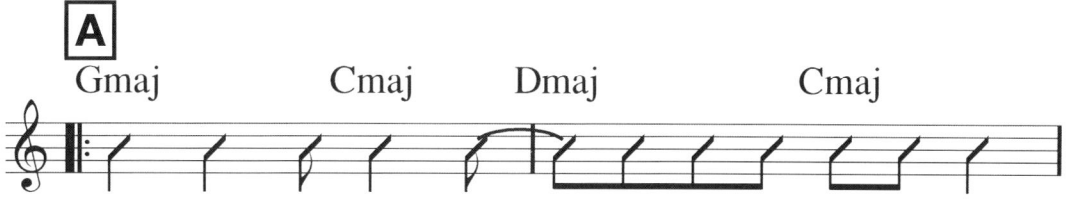

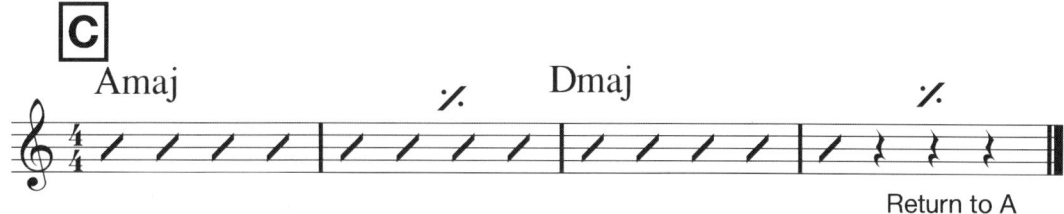

Return to A

R.

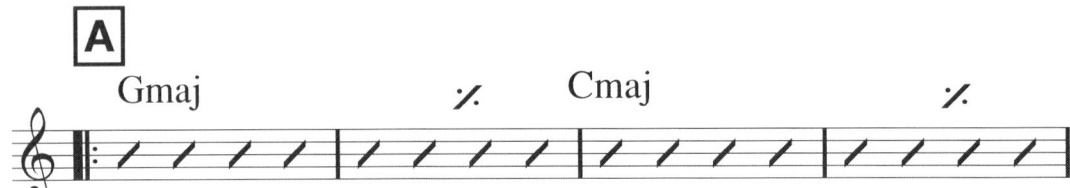

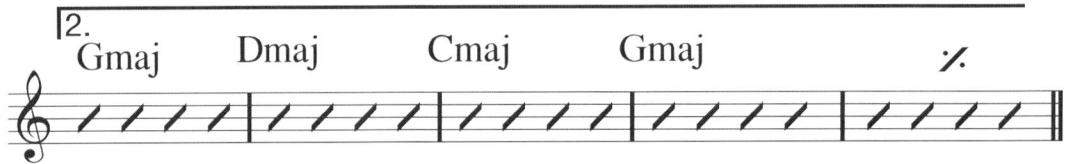

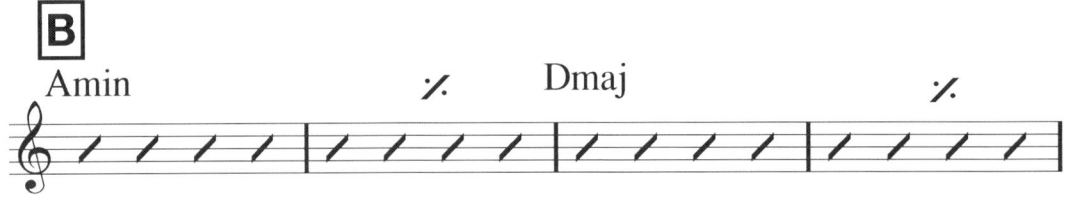

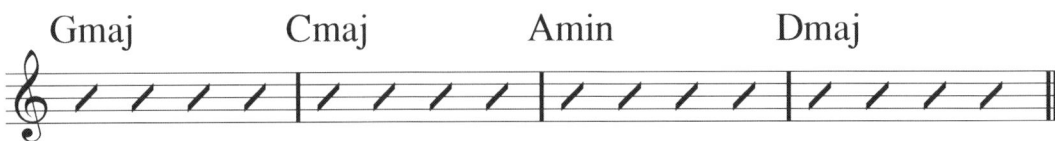

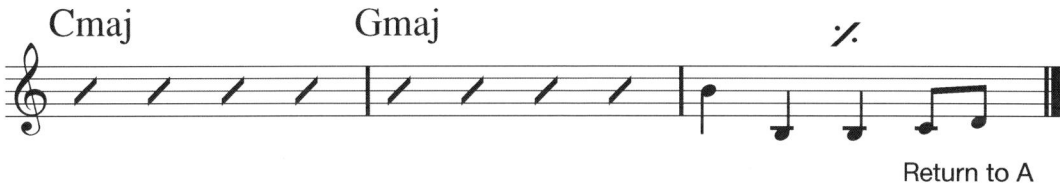

Return to A

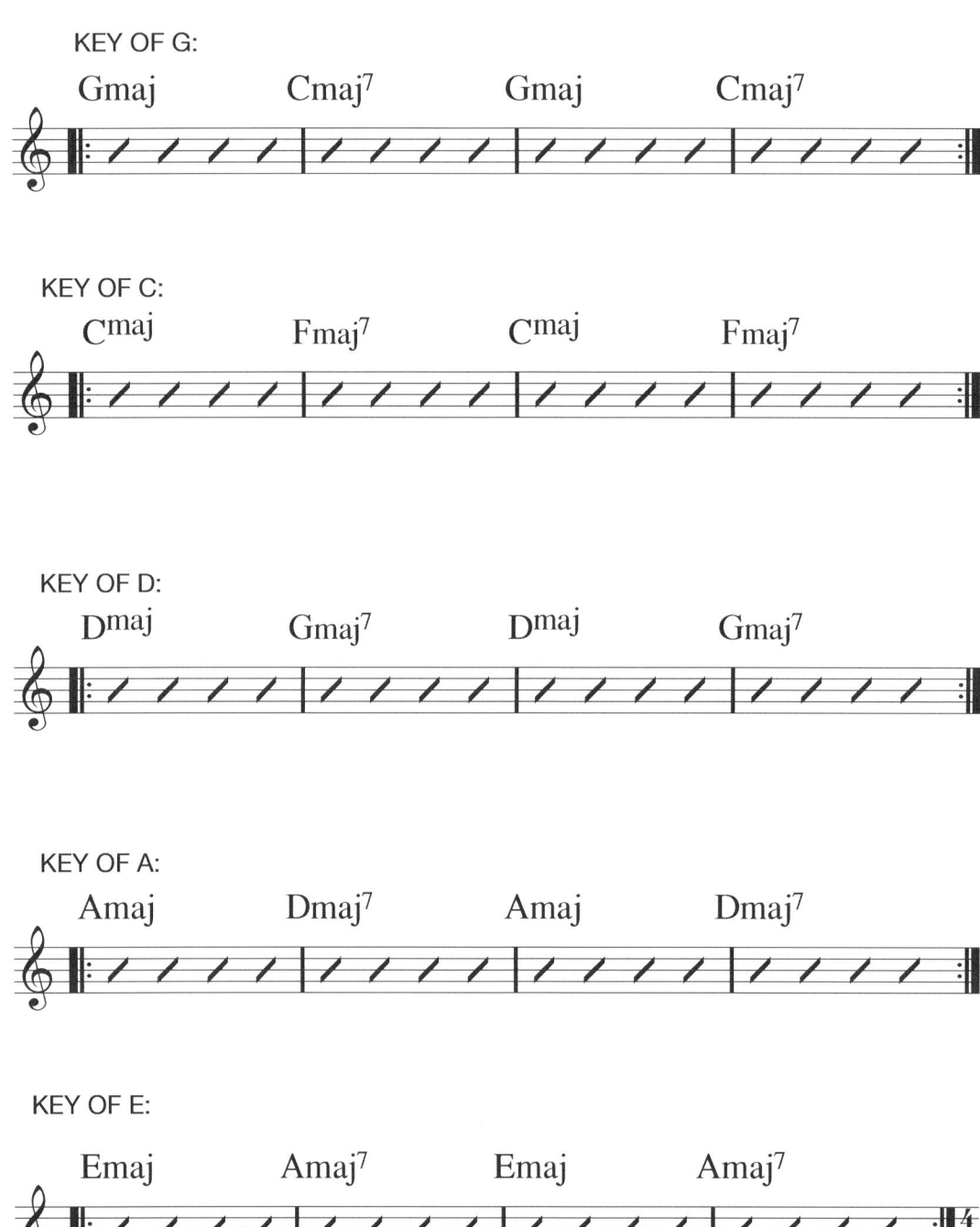

C. Rds

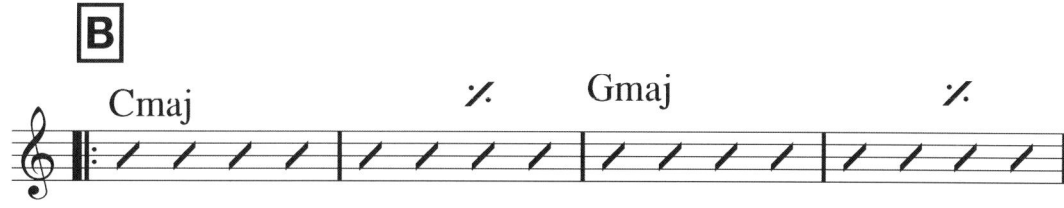

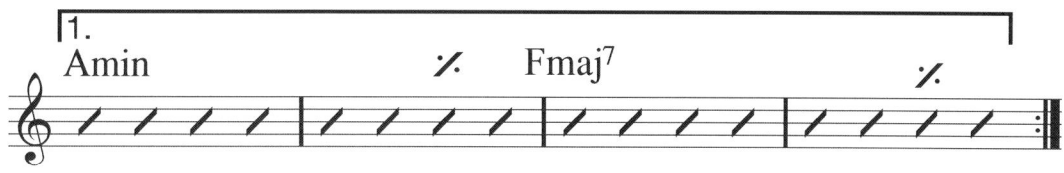

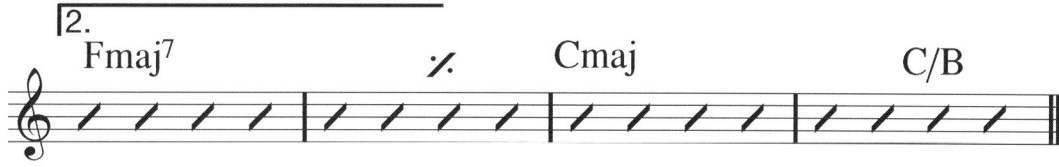

172

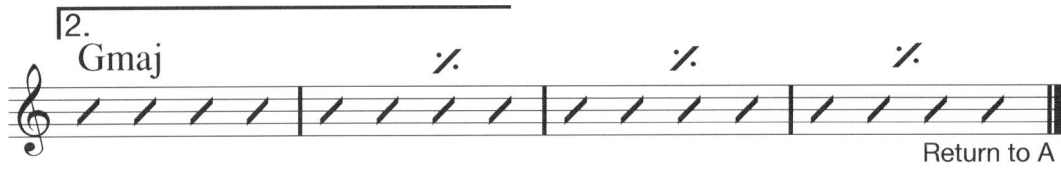

Return to A

R.M.H.

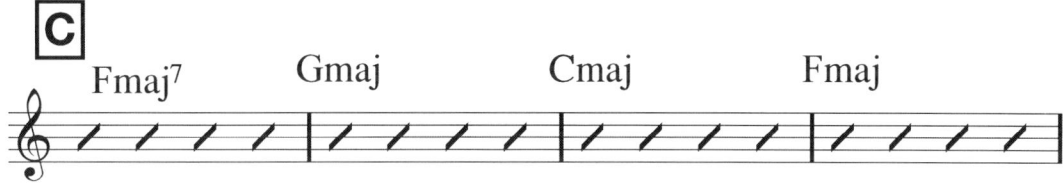

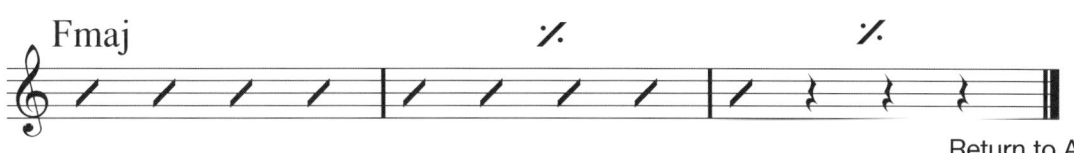

Return to A

T.N.T.D. O. D. D.

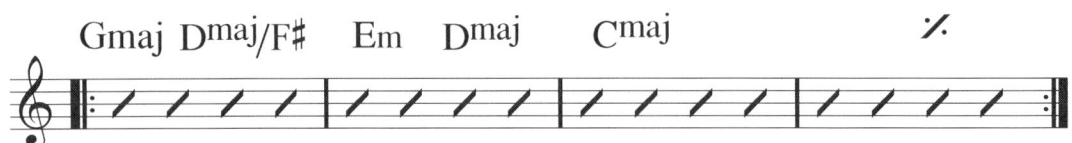
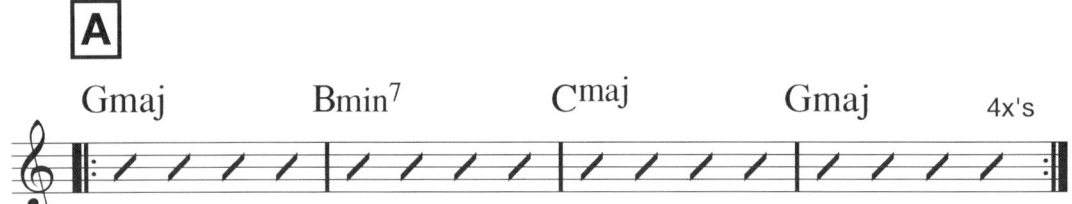

A Gracing Maze

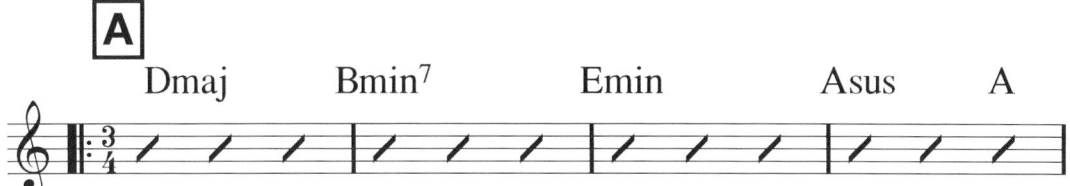

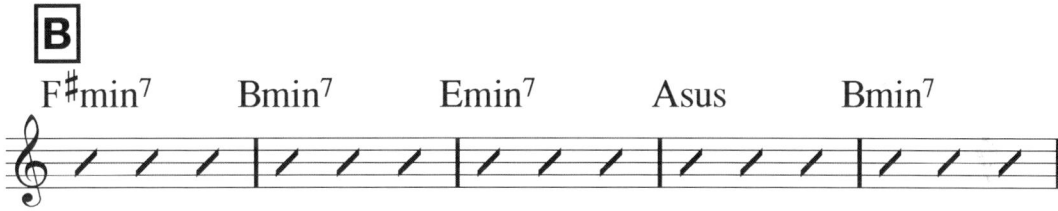
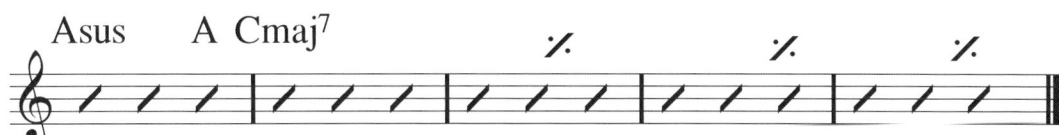

INDEX

*If you learn music,
you'll learn most
all there is to know.*

- Edgar Casey -

Reference Guide

This index is grouped for quick practice reference.

Fundamentals:
    Holding The Guitar 2
    Left Hand 4
    Right Hand 5
    Picking 6
    Tuning 7
    Note Names 8
    Time Signature 9
    Notation Values 13
    Intervals 16
    Dynamics 20
    Counting 23
    Open-String Groupings 27
    String Names 30
    Counting 1/4, 1/8, 1/16 32-35
    Chord Transition Formulas 85

Chords:
    Power Chords 80
    Eight Open-Position Chords - *vertical alignment* 83
    Six Major Chords 88
    Nine Open-Position Chords - *horizontal alignment* 106
    Special Case Chords - *vertical alignment* 111
    Special Case Chords - *horizontal alignment* 113
    Introduction To Barre Chords 114
    Bmaj, B7 Bmin Chords 124

Chord Theory & Composition:
    Mod Chord Theory - *diatonic harmony* 97
    Basic Notation vi
    Basic Song Forms viii

About:
    Metronomes 35
    Music 63

Rhythm Guitar:
    Open-String Groupings 21
    Graduated Rhythms 19
    Rhythm Guitar #1 18
    Rhythm Guitar #2 - *basic strum patterns* 28
    Rhythm Guitar #3 - *folk strum 1* 95
    Rhythm Guitar #4 - *rock ballad* 103
    Rhythm Guitar #5 - *boom chick* 111
    Rhythm Workout #1 - *quarters & eights* 117

Practice Progressions:
    #1 - *8 Open-Position Chords* 91
    #2 - *I-IV-V Chords* 99
    #3 - *Common Chord Patterns* 104
    #4 - *9 Open-Position Chords* 107
    #5 - *Special Case Chords* 113
    #6 - *Rhythm Workouts* 122

Scales:
Open-Position:
    C Major 46
    Chromatic Scale 61
    E Minor Pentatonic 65
    E Blues Scale 71

Speed Studies:
    C Major Scale 57
    Chromatic Scale 61
    E Minor Pentatonic 67
    E Blues Scale 73

Right Hand Studies:
- Right Hand Position 5
- Holding The Pick 6
- Dividing String Groups 22
- Counting Even Rhythms 23
- Finding Home Base 26
- Counting 1/4 Notes 32
- Counting 1/8 Notes 34
- Counting 1/16 Notes 35
- Picking Across 2 Adjacent Strings 38
- Picking Across 3 Adjacent Strings 41
- Right Hand Left Hand Subdivisions - *C major scale* 49-57
- Chromatic Scale Study 61
- Rhythm Guitar Workout #1 117-120
- Finger Picking 127-135

Sample Practice Sessions

This is to be used as is or as a general template for practice. Each session can be lengthened or shortened proportionally.

Beginning 1 hour Practice Session:
Open-string strums: 5 min
  Break: 5 min
Scales: 15 min
  Break: 5 min
Chords: 15 min
  Break: 5 min
Tunes: 10 min

Intermediate 1 hour Practice Session:
Scales: 20 min
  Break: 5 min
Chords: 20 min
  Break: 5 min
Tunes: 10 min

Advanced 2 hour Practice Session:
Scales: 30 min
  Break: 5 min
Chords: 30 min
  Break: 5 min
Tunes: 50 min

Basic Notation Practices for Song Writing

Repeat Signs:

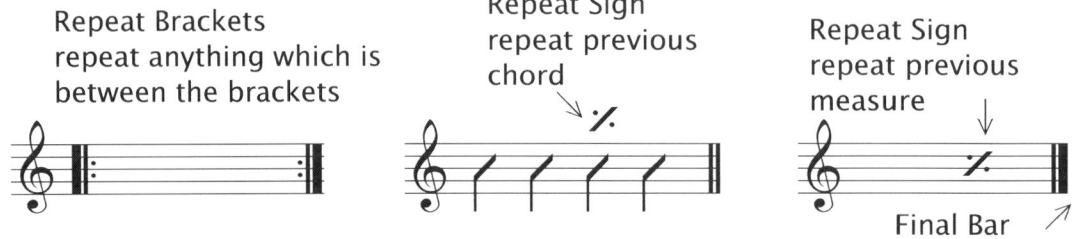

C **Rehearsal Mark**: for marking Song Sections.

Slash Notaion for Chords:

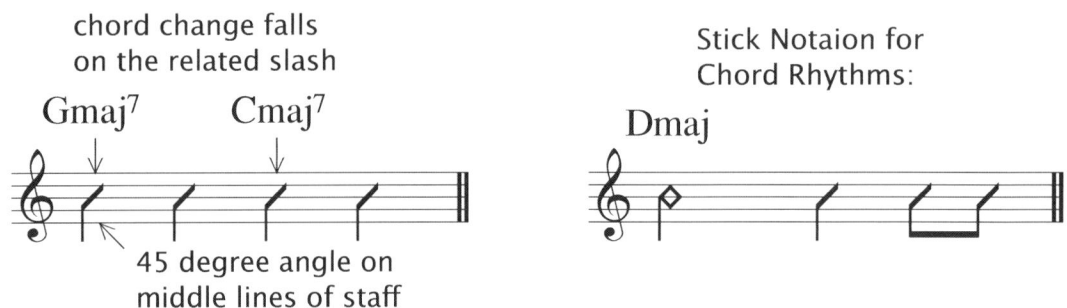

Play 1st end, repeat and take the 2nd end.

vii

Take an Intro. = Play 4-8 measures Introduction taken from first or last 8 bars of tune. Sometimes can start on the B section.
From The Top = From the beginning of the tune including intro.
Play the Head = Play the A section of the tune.
Play the Bridge = Play the B section of the tune.

Simile = similar

⊓ = Down Stroke

V = Up Stroke

⊓ V = Alternate down/up Stroke

⊕ = Coda

𝄋 = Sign

D.C. = Dal Capa - Return to the beginning of tune.

D.S. = Dal Segno - Return to the sign. 𝄋

f = Fortissimo (Loud)
p = Pianissimo (Soft)
m = Moderate (Medium/Normal)

4 Basic Strum Patterns:

a)
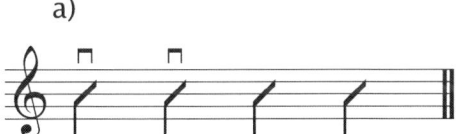

b)
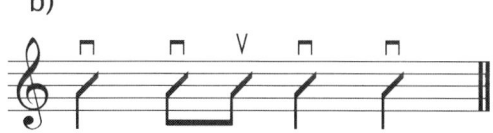

c)
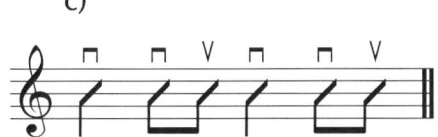

d)
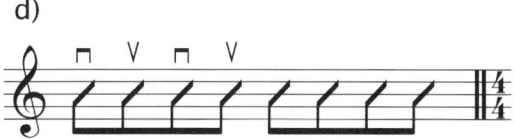

SONG FORM #1

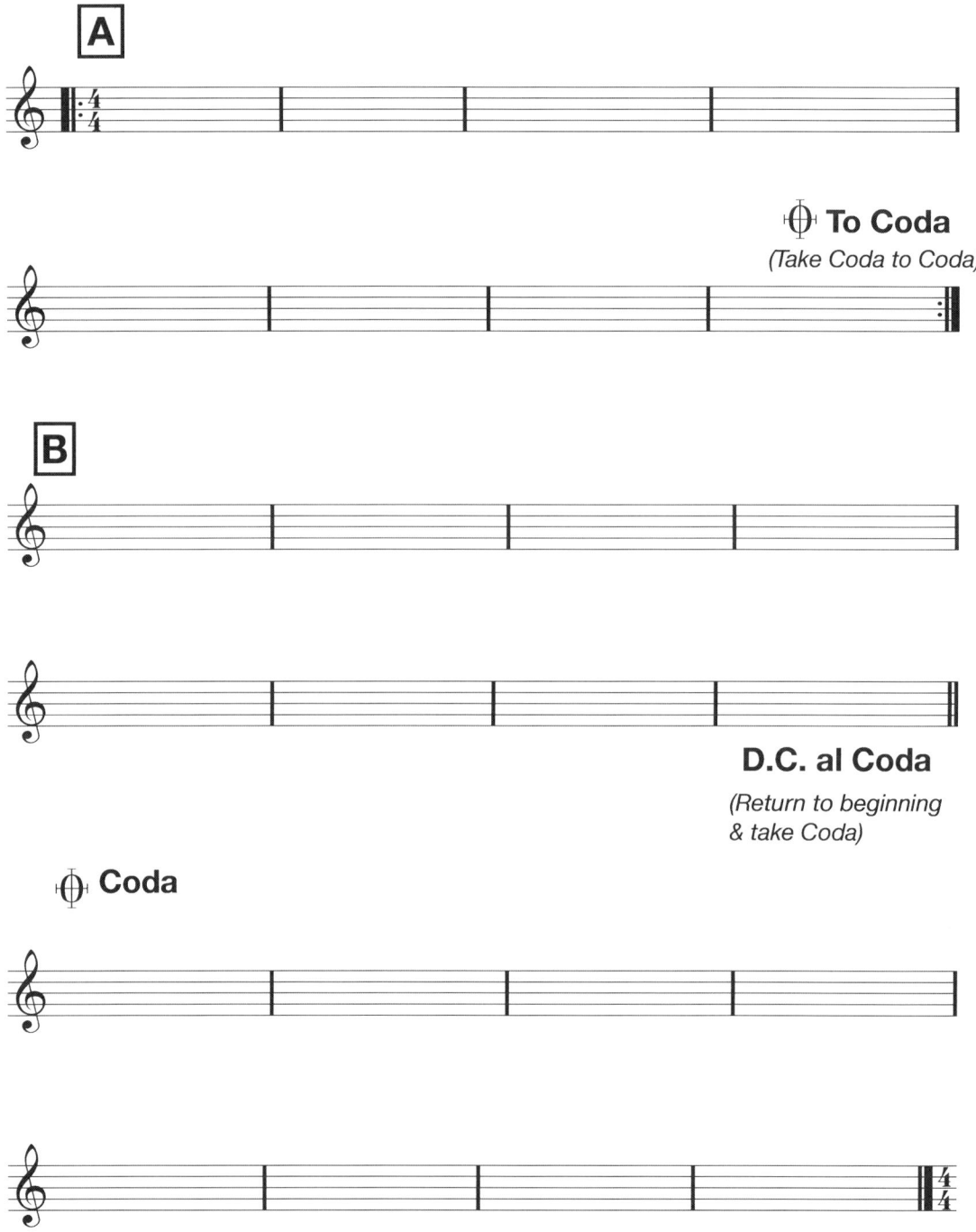

SONG FORM #2

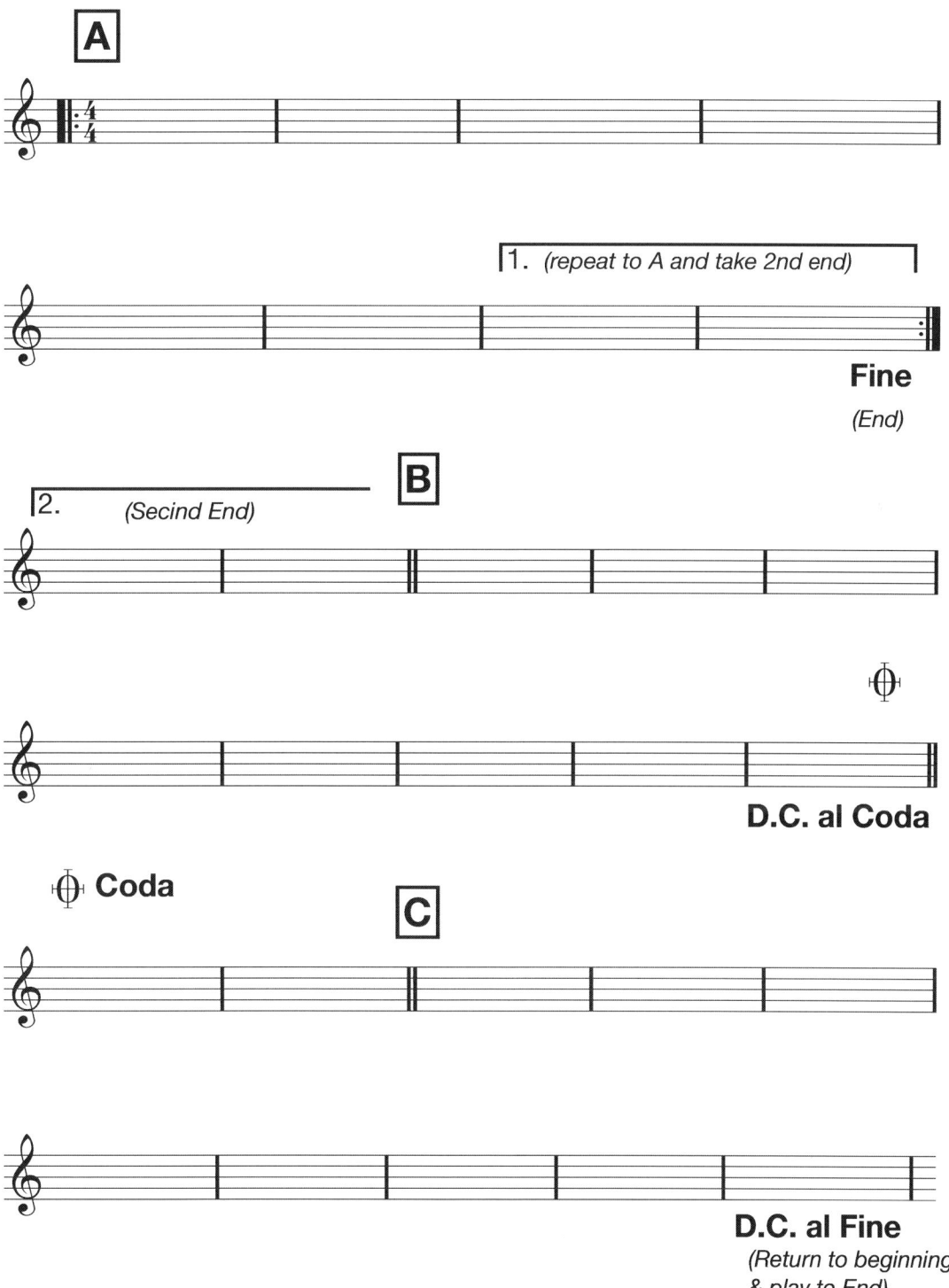

OTHER AVAILABLE TITLES

CD: Todd Ferris Mosby
Indian Music

CD: Mosby Group
Missouri Music

CD: Mosby Group
East West

BK: Mosby Music Method
Classical Studies For Contemporary Players

BK: Mosby Music Method
Acoustic Guitar Techniques For Songwriters Volume 2

www.mosbymusicgroup.com

Made in the USA
Lexington, KY
03 February 2013